The AFRICA
RESPO
ADJUSTMENT OR TRANSFORMATION

Introduction by Bade Onimode

Proceedings of the IFAA workshop to review :

The World Bank report
"Sub-Saharan Africa : from Crisis to Sustainable Growth – A Long-term Perspective Study"

The Uruguay Round of GATT

The Fraser Report on Africa's Commodity Problems

Held January 1991 at the
United Nations Economic Commission For Africa (ECA)
Addis Ababa, Ethiopia.

The African Response - Adjustment or Transformation
was first published by the Institute for African Alternatives,
23 Bevenden Street, London N1 6BH, United Kingdom, in 1992

Edited by Mary Turok
Designed and typeset by Pascale Vassie
Printed and bound by Billings Book Plan

A catalogue record for this book is available from the British Library
ISBN 1-870425-32-4

Acknowledgements

IFAA wishes to express appreciation to ICCO - Interchurch Organization for Development Cooperation, one of the funders of the Addis Ababa Conference, who made the publication of the proceedings possible.

Contents

About the Contributors

Dr. Salim Ahmed Salim is Secretary General of the Organization of African Unity

Dr. Bade Onimode is Professor of Economics at the University of Ibadan, Nigeria and Chairperson of the Council of IFAA

Ketso Gordham is an economist with the Economic Policy Department of the African National Congress in Johannesburg, South Africa

Bertha Koda is a Senior Lecturer in the Institute of Development Studies at the University of Dar es Salaam, Tanzania

Dr. Wilfred W. Asombang is a consultant at the Economic Commission for Africa in Addis Ababa, Ethiopia

Dr. L.A. Osunde is the General Secretary of the Nigerian Labour Congress

Ben Turok is Director of the Institute for African Alternatives (IFAA) and is based in Johannesburg, South Africa

Emy Siganga represented the Association of African Women in Research and Development in Kenya

Dr. Abdoulaye Bathily is Professor of History at the University of Dakar, Senegal

John Karimu is attached to CUSO in The Gambia

Ernest Maganya is a Senior Lecturer at the Institute of Development Studies, University of Dar es Salaam, Tanzania

Sam Orio is an economist working for the Environment Liaison Centre International in Nairobi, Kenya

Dr. Mohammed Nureldin Hussain is associate Professor at the University of Gezira, Sudan

Hassan Sunmonu is Secretary General of the Organisation of African Trade Union Unity, based in Accra, Ghana

Chakravarthi Raghavan is an Indian journalist and GATT observer in Geneva, Switzerland

Dr. Mohammed Suliman is Deputy Director of IFAA and Head of the Environment at IFAA, London

Martin Khor Kok Peng is a leading Third World Network activist and editor of 'Third World Economics'.

Dr. S. Tomori is Professor of Economics at the University of Lagos, Nigeria and is President of the African Economic Association

Dr. A. Dirar is Director of the Economic, Development and Co-operation Department of the OAU

Tchouta Moussa is Deputy Executive Secretary of the UN Economic Commission For Africa (ECA)

Abbreviations

AAF-SAP	African Alternative Framework to Structural Adjustment Programmes for Socio-Economic Recovery and Transformation.
ACGSF	African Credit Guarantee Scheme Fund
ACP	African, Caribbean and Pacific
ADP	African Development Project
APPER	African Priority Programme for Economic Recovery
BIS	Bank for International Settlements
CBN	Central Bank of Nigeria
CCM	Chama cha Mapinduzi
ECA	Economic Commission for Africa
ERP	Economic Recovery Programme
EEC	European Economic Community
EMS	European Monetary System
FAO	Food and Agricultural Organisation
GATT	General Agreement on Trade and Tariffs
GDP	Gross Domestic Product
GEPC	Ghana Export Promotion Council
GRATIS	Ghana Regional Appropriate Technology Industrial Service
IDA	International Development Association
IFAA	Institute for African Alternatives
ILO	International Labour Organisation
IMF	International Monetary Fund
IBRD	International Bank for Reconstruction and Development (World Bank)
IRDP	Integrated Rural Development Project
ITO	International Trade Organisation
ITTU	Intermediate Technology Transfer Unit
LDC	Less Developed Country
LNDC	Lesotho National Development Corporation
LIBOR	London Inter-Bank Offered Rate
MAN	Manufacturers Association of Nigeria
MAMSER	Mass Mobilisation for Self-reliance, Economic Recovery and Social Justice

MIGA	Multilateral Investment Guarantee Agency
MNC	Multinational Corporation
NAFPP	National Accelerated Food Production Plan
NANS	National Association of Nigerian Students
NACB	Nigerian Agricultural and Cooperative Bank
NATO	North Atlantic Treaty Organisation
NESP	National Economic Survival Programme
NIC	Newly Industrialised Country
NIDEO	New International Democratic Economic Order
NIEO	New International Economic Order
NLC	Nigerian Labour Congress
NODC	Non-Oil Developing Country
NRC	Nigerian Republic Convention
NUTA	National Union of Tanganyikan Workers
OAU	Organisation of African Unity
ODA	Official Development Assistance
OECD	Organisation for European Cooperation and Development
OFN	Operation Feed the Nation
OPEC	Organisation of Petroleum Exporting Countries
PNDC	Provisional National Defence Council
PTA	Preferential Trade Area
RBDA	River Basin Development Association
SADCC	Southern African Development Coordinating Conference
SAP	Structural Adjustment Programme
SDA	Social Dimension of Adjustment
SDP	Social Democratic Party
SDR	Special Drawing Right
SHLS	Small Holder Loan Scheme
SSA	Sub-Saharan Africa
TANU	Tanganyika African National Union
TCC	Technology Consultancy Centre
TFL	Tanganyika Federation of Labour
TNC	Transnational Corporation
TRIMS	Trade Related Investment Measures
TRIPS	Trade Related Property Rights
UN	United Nations
UNCTAD	UN Conference on Trade and Development
UNICEF	UN Children's fund
UN-PAAERD	UN Programme of Action for African Economic Recovery and Development
USAID	United States Agency for International Development

Introduction

This volume contains the edited papers and speeches by participants from across Africa at a rather special conference. It was convened by the Institute for African Alternatives (IFAA) but the staff of the United Nations Commission for Africa (ECA) and the Organisation of African Unity (OAU) played an active part throughout. The ECA provided conference facilities and many of their senior staff chaired sessions and made important interventions.

The opening address was delivered on behalf of the OAU by its Secretary General, Salim A. Salim, and the conference was closed by Tchouta Moussa, Deputy Executive Secretary of the ECA.

The most important feature of the conference was the extraordinary consensus that characterised all sessions , and the strength of feeling about the external pressures currently being exerted on Africa by the present undemocratic world economic order and its institutions.

The three documents under examination were seen to be of seminal importance. They reflected the approaches now being adopted in the North towards Africa and the harsh treatment accorded to the continent on the world stage.

The Long-term Perspective Study (LTPS) of the World Bank, the Fraser Report on Africa's Commodity Problems and the Uruguay Round of GATT were carefully examined in turn. While each has particular concerns their overall perspectives are the same.

Africa is being accorded unfavourable economic terms by the lending institutions and by trading organs. Thus Africa continues to be plagued by external debt, by expensive loans and by disastrous terms or trade and exchange rates. This constitutes exploitation of the South by the North. At the same time Africa is being marginalised politically and effectively excluded from decision making in the international arena.

Africa's governments and formal institutions are having to face up to these realities and develop alternatives. The ECA's African Alternative Framework to Structural Adjustment Programmes (AAF-SAP) was one such initiative. The NGO's African Charter for Popular Participation in Development was another. IFAA too has been involved in the construction of alternatives for Africa. There is an urgent need for all similar bodies to pursue the same objective.

WORKSHOP STATEMENT

1. This Workshop was attended by representatives of the academic community, trade unions, non-government organisations from several African countries and foreign observers and was held in the context of the serious threat posed to the economies, environment and sovereignty of African countries by the World Bank's publication titled "Sub-Saharan Africa: from Crisis to Sustainable Growth - A Long-term Perspective Study (LTPS)", the Uruguay Round of GATT and the Fraser Report on Africa's Commodity Problems.

2. The Workshop noted the admission by the World Bank in its LTPS of the failure of its sponsored policies over the last three decades and of Structural Adjustment Programmes (SAPs) imposed on African countries over the last decade. The Bank has come to accept some of the concerns and policy directions of the OAU, ECA, IFAA and other organisations and critics, and has borrowed their language heavily. The areas of this emerging agreement include: the need for adjustment with growth, human-centred development, regional co-operation and integration, and democratic participation. We, however, note that this apparent consensus does not extend to the means of achieving these goals nor to concrete policies and programmes of action for the implementation of the areas of agreement.

3. We reject the spurious assumptions in the LTPS which are not borne out by the facts. They include the suggestion that Africa has no long-term development perspective; that the existing Structural Adjustment Programmes (SAPs) should continue as new generation (SAPs); that African governments should withdraw into the background in the recovery and development of the region; that reliance on market forces with free or competitive pricing is the best way forward for Africa; that greater co-operation between African and industrialised countries on current terms can ensure sustainable development; that the informal sector should be relied upon heavily for industrialisation and general development of African countries; that peasant or small-holder agriculture should be the major basis for transformation of Africa's agriculture

and that development in the social services should be based on cost-recovery or market prices in education, health, transport, etc.

4. We reaffirm that Africa has over the years prepared its own long-term development plans such as the Lagos Plan of Action for Africa's Development from 1980 to the year 2000 (LPA) and the ECA's Long-term Perspective from 1980 to the year 2008. More recently in 1989, the African Alternative Framework to Structural Adjustment Programmes for Socio-economic Recovery and Transformation (AAF-SAP) was also prepared and adopted by African countries. We note with concern the World Bank's persistent opposition to and rejection of these African programmes in preference to its own which are less informed, less relevant and which have failed disastrously, like its on-going SAPs.

5. We, therefore, call-upon our governments to abandon the World Bank/IMF imposed SAPs and LTPSs and to take urgent steps to implement their own programmes - AAF-SAP and LPA. We also call-upon the IMF, the World Bank and the international community to respect the independence and sovereignty of African countries in choosing their path of development. They should, instead, support Africa's initiatives as claimed in the LTPS rather than displace them.

6. The workshop condemns the call in the LTPS for 'new generation SAP's'in spite of the catastrophic failure of on-going SAP's and the fact that African countries have produced an alternative to SAP in the form of the Afircan Alternative Framework to Structural Adjustment Programmes for Socio-economic Recovery and Tranformation (AAF-SAP). The suggestion in the LTPS that SAP's are still evolving means that the World Bank is making African countries guinea pigs for costly policy experiments. We condemn this and call on the World Bank, the IMF and other multilateral agencies to support Africa's legitimate and informed initatives in the design and implementation of adjustment and development programmes as proclaimed repeatedly in the LTPS.

7. We also feel very concerned about the sectoral policies and programmes in the LTPS that are based mostly on free market forces and the total opening up of African economies along with the virtual denial of a significant role for the state. In industry, for example, we disagree with the trend towards de-industrialisation, denial of state participation in promoting intermediate and capital-goods industries, excessive reliance on the informal sector and

transnational corporations and the call for generalised devaluation that has led to factory closures, capacity under-utilization, pernicious inflation and massive retrenchment. In agriculture, we also disagree with the denial of agricultural support policies in Africa though these are being used massively in the industrialised countries; the excessive reliance on peasant production to transform Africa's agriculture without major efforts on co-operatives; dissolution of Marketing Boards with excessive reliance on free markets as well as the conflict between food and export crop production. We maintain that it is impossible to rely on market pricing or cost recovery user charges in social services like health and education for the promotion of human resources development. This conflicts with any commitment to equity and the protection of the poor as claimed in the LTPS.

8. The Workshop, therefore, rejects the LTPS strategic agenda for the 1990s emanating from this incorrect diagnosis of the problem, and finds the proposal of a "Global Coalition for Africa (GCA)" particularly paternalistic and unacceptable. We know that Africa has already produced its own strategic agenda for the 1990's in the form of the revitalization of the LPA and the implementation of AAF- SAP. The World Bank should therefore stop wasting scarce resources in duplicating these more relevant African programmes and join forces with the African countries in implementing them.

9. The Workshop noted with concern the secrecy and undemocratic nature of the negotiations in the Uruguay Round of GATT and the marginalization of African countries and their organizations. We reject the attempt by the industrialized countries to impose new trade policies and practices that will eliminate the development principle and the right to protect infant industries as in the present GATT. The proposals in the Uruguay Round will impose an estimated net loss of about US$ 3 billion annually on African countries. It will also impose loss of access to foreign markets, especially for agricultural and textile products, and recolonize African coun tries through the removal of Africa's right to control transnational corporations, foreign investment, technology, banking, insurance and travel, and the African environment. We condemn the greed of the industrialized countries in their attempt, through the GATT negotiations to further impoverish and recolonize Africa and the rest of the Third World. For these reasons Africa should reject the Uruguay Round of GATT negotiations. We strongly support the activities of the OAU, the Economic Commision for Africa (ECA) and other non-governmental organisations whose efforts in improving the negotiating capacity of African

countries have helped in resisting the unjust and exploitative proposals of the industrialized countries.

10. The Workshop endorses Africa's Common Position on the Fraser Report on Africa's Commodity Problems. We reject the Fraser Report as excessively conservative, partisan and inconsistent with Africa's repeated position on its deteriorating export trade problems.

The Report is a repetition of World Bank analysis and prescriptions on Africa's external trade. It is an unacceptable attempt to return Africa to the 1960s and to the failed concentration on so-called traditional export commodities that have been facing reduced foreign markets due to protectionism and synthetic substitution for raw materials. Its suggestion that the causes of Africa's trade problems are only internal is false and its recommendations on export diversification, compensatory financing and additional international financial support for Africa's exports are too general, conservative and grossly inadequate. We, therefore, call-upon the United Nations to take urgent measures to implement the more relevant policy recommendations in the African Common Position on the Fraser Report.

11. The Workshop appeals to the African intellectual community, non-governmental organisations, trade unions and the patriotic business community, women, youth and students to lobby and assist our governments in exposing the intrigues behind World Bank's LTPS, the Uruguay Round of GATT and the Fraser report. We urge them to reject these documents because they will undermine Africa's recovery and development. We also call upon them to forge a United Front or Regional Coalition of all social forces in support of the progressive work of the OAU, ECA and ADB in promoting and defending Africa's development and sovereignty.

12. The workshop, however, notes with concern the disparity between the pronouncements and commitments of our governments at national and international levels and their policy actions. We also note that in some instances, this dichotomy is due to the threats, intimidation and blackmail of external forces. We therefore call for popular participation in governance to counter external blackmail and to promote full democratization and effective accountability as being the best conditions for ensuring rapid recovery with structural transformation. This must be the driving force of Africa's agenda for the 1990s and beyond.

OPENING ADDRESS

Dr. Salim Ahmed Salim, Secretary General of the Organization of African Unity

We understand that this Conference is to deliberate on the General Agreement on Tariff and Trade (GATT) and the World Bank Long-term Perspective Study. It is being held not because the issues to be raised are new but because of our belief that this forum will help to further underline several of Africa's preoccupations in the international, commercial and economic fields; the need for increased external financial and technical assistance to overcome the debt burden and the economic crisis; and to lay the foundations for the evolution of endogenous self-reliant and self-sustaining economic development.

As the distinguished participants are well aware, contemporary international commercial relations are essentially governed by the rules and principles established within the GATT. The basic aim of GATT is to liberalise world trade and in the process contribute to the improvement of the welfare of the peoples of the world through the growth of non-discriminatory world trade and economic development. Some 30 African countries are contracting parties to the GATT and about 10 more apply the GATT on a de facto basis.

We at the OAU have been following very closely the progress of the current Uruguay Round of negotiations, although the OAU has been persistently refused Observer Status within the forums of the GATT. However, we have managed to send representatives to all recent meetings and to press for the enhancement of the negotiating capacity of OAU Member States. Above all our Permanent Delegation in Geneva continues to monitor developments on a daily basis from outside the GATT forums.

As a result of this experience we can safely conclude that GATT negotiations are not conceived to address Africa's problems in the international commercial arena. The African countries concluded that the package presented to the Brussels meeting in December 1990, would almost certainly result in net losses to African countries in all areas, particularly in access to markets, agricultural negotiations, services, trade related investment measures (TRIMS), trade related intellectual property rights (TRIPS), rights to protect their economies and balance of payments under the relevant Articles of the Agreement, etc. Consequently, the African countries informed the Contracting Parties in their statement that the package would be acceptable to them only if, I quote:

(a) all developed countries would improve the access to markets for African countries, including preferential access, so as to compensate them for the erosion of existing preferences;

(b) the transitional mechanism on textiles and clothing would ensure that no new restrictions would be imposed on African countries and existing restrictions and restraints would be phased out before the expiry of the transitional period;

(c) the results of agricultural negotiations would provide differential and more favourable treatment to (i) enable African countries to continue to protect and complement programmes to encourage agricultural and rural development while obtaining preferential access to world markets, and (ii) to compensate any negative effect on net food imports;

(d) the negotiations result in the acceptance of meaningful disciplines to prevent the export of domestically prohibited goods and hazardous substances to the African continent;

(e) special and differential treatment were established to allow small suppliers from African countries to be exempted from safeguard measures or countervailing and anti-dumping duties;

(f) there were provisions in any agreement on intellectual property rights which would enable African countries to be exempted from any higher obligations with respect to norms and standards in view of their low level of economic development, or would allow them to adopt measures deemed necessary to alleviate poverty, to protect public health and nutrition, and to promote public interest in sectors of vital importance to their socio-economic and technological development;

(g) any agreement on TRIMS did not include provisions that would limit African countries right to promote development objectives or to counter anti-competitive practices through investment measures, so long as such measures did not cause restrictive or distorting effects on trade;

(h) a multilateral framework agreement on trade in services, under which any liberalization commitments by African countries would be made in the light of progress in the strengthening of their domestic service sectors, and the means they are given to this end (such as transfer of technology and conditions imposed on foreign suppliers), and their being granted effective access to world markets, including the movement of labour; and which would not impede their efforts toward greater regional and sub-regional integration;

(i) provisions to provide free and unrestricted access to markets for goods and services from the least-developed countries, without their having to enter into reciprocal commitments of any form.

Only when all these "ifs" had been adequately addressed would the package be acceptable.

You all know that the negotiations could not be concluded as anticipated in December 1990. But, given the undemocratic nature of the GATT system and the "green room" negotiatons procedures, there is little hope that the outcome will be substantially improved to accommodate the interests of developing countries, and particularly Africa which has the majority of the least developed countries. Judging from press reports it seems that the negotiators are not giving these issues the priority they deserve. The only way the third world can get any benefits or indeed minimize the damage to their economies is by standing solidly together in a united front and refusing to accept a package that does not cover their concerns. I am aware of the tremendous pressures applied on some major trading third world countries, particularly by the US, using the powers given by Congress to the US trade representatives to adopt unilateral sanctions and to request voluntary restrictions and even to blacklist countries, in clear violation of the GATT Articles. That notwithstanding, the only way to get any negotiating weight is through unity of the third world.

As you obviously know, Africa is heavily dependent on the export of commodities and if it has any grudge with the international trading system, it is because of such perennial problems as: the meagre prices paid for commodities African countries export, prices which are not commensurate with their production, marketting and transportation costs; the persistently unstable and erratic price fluctuations resulting in declining and undependable external revenues; reduced volume of exports due to Africa's loss of market share; problems posed by subsidies and protectionist policies applied by the developed market economy countries which dominate the GATT negotiations.

Another problem which is hardly addressed is the threat posed by modern technology and biotechnology to Africa's commodities in order to discourage industrial processing which improves the value-added content of raw materials.

It is against this background that we should view any international trade negotiations with respect to trade in goods. If they are not designed to address these problems, then in our view Africa's interest is not covered. That is why, in spite of the on-going Uruguay Round Negotiations, in May 1988 the OAU called upon the UN Secretary General to constitute a High Level Expert Group on African Commodity Problems. That group was constituted and its findings have been published in the report entitled "AFRICA'S COMMODITY PROBLEMS - TOWARDS A SOLUTION".

The OAU's response to that report is contained in the paper entitled "AFRICA'S COMMON POSITION ON THE REPORT - AFRICA'S COMMODITY PROBLEMS TOWARDS A SOLUTION", which analysed the report and presented a number of concrete proposals for action. These documents were considered by the UN General Assembly in December 1990 and a resolution was adopted requesting the SG to take a number of actions in close consultation with the OAU.

Let me now turn to the Long-term Perspective Study of the World Bank and see how all these issues relate to it. In our view the relevance lies in that the sustainable and equitable growth stategy proposed by the Bank uses trade as a major means for securing these aims. The strategy is based on a 4 –5 per cent annual growth target. It stresses that the primary source of this growth should be agricultural production which is targeted to expand annually at 4 per cent to generate food requirements and foreign exchange for development. The strategy also calls on Africa to raise domestic savings and investment and aims at creating an enabling environment.It calls for the introduction or strengthening of incentives to encourage production and private initiative.

While calling for increased agricultural production the Long-term Perspective Study recognises that overseas markets on which African agricultural commodities depend will remain highly competitive and that long-term price trends could not be expected to improve. In the light of such a scenario the study recommends, inter alia, that African countries would need to diversify their production base and seek out other market outlets. Above all, the Bank recommends that "Greater regional integration would particularly help expand trade within Africa in agricultural products, especially food". The study goes on to call for the development of the industrial sector in response to market opportunities and asserts that African leaders have rightly placed priority on enlarging markets through regional integration.

With the impact of the Structural Adjustment Programmes (SAP) of the IMF and World Bank, which are being widely implemented in member states of the OAU, and bearing in mind the study's own recommendations for sustained industrial growth based in part on a broadly based expansion of domestic demand for local manufactured goods, it has been recognised that there is a conflict of policy in that SAP pose a crippling threat to domestic industry by the massive importation of foreign manufactured goods under the liberalised trade and import policies that African countries are made to pursue under SAP.

Nevertheless, the contents of the Long-term Perspective Study of the World Bank have gone a long way in the search for alternative policy instruments for Africa's socio-economic development – and I am glad to put this on record . Unlike the infamous Berg Report, the "Accelerated Development for Africa - Agenda for Action" published by the Bank in 1981 soon after the OAU adopted the Lagos Plan of Action and the Final Act of Lagos, the Long-term Perspective Study has come round to accepting economic integration as the major long-term tool for Africa's socio-economic transformation and development. However, it is important to note that the Perspective Study came into being as a result of the concerted efforts of African countries, their organisations and friends to persuade the Bank that the traditional SAPs are doing more harm than good to Africa's long term development. There is still strong resistance within the Bank to departing from its old ways and there is therefore a need to continue the pressure and the dialogue with the Bank in order to implement the positive recommendations in the study and to translate some of its recommendations into operational programmes through changes in the SAP programmes. We should not forget that the study is a programme that can only be taken up if Africa and its friends continue the pressure for reform to the SAPs or their replacement with more realistic and long term programmes, well backed by required resources.

In view of the decision of the Heads of State and Government of the OAU to establish an African Economic Community, the draft Treaty of which should be signed by June 1991, and bearing in mind the African Common Position on the Report on African Commodity Problems and Africa's Alternative to Structural Adjustment (AAF-SAP) and the Declaration of the last summit of the OAU, African countries and institutions should strengthen their resolve and efforts to convince the Bank to share their prespectives and goals and bring to their support the required resources and knowhow.

I, therefore, hope that this Conference, organised by the Institute for African Alternatives, will be in a position to recommend a practical and implementable set of policies and measures, not only to OAU Member States but also to the international community, especially the international financial institutions.

THE OBJECTIVES OF THE WORKSHOP

Professor Bade Onimode,
Chairperson of the Council of IFAA

This workshop is being organized by the Institute for African Alternatives on three very topical questions: The World Bank's recent major policy publication on Africa titled: "Sub-Saharan Africa: From Crisis to Sustainable Growth (A Long-term Perspective Study)", the Fraser Report on Africa's Commodity Problems, commissioned by the U.N. Secretary General , and the Uruguay Round of GATT and moves towards a new world trading system.

Firstly, we should note that the World Bank's Long-term Perspective Study (LTPS) was launched with a fanfare across Africa in December 1989. In July 1990 there was a media conference which many of us saw as an attempt to start implementing the ideas in the LTPS.

The conference made two main suggestions. Firstly, the possibility of establishing a global coalition for Africa, as recommended on pages 15 and 193-5 of the LTPS, which was supposed to be formed between African leaders and foreign development partners. Its major responsibility would be to promote general agreement on overall strategies for Africa's long-term development, in addition to offering guidance on how Africa should go about the process of development.

The second suggestion from this major conference, which has not got very far but which we understand is still being pushed, is the idea of getting African countries to start preparing national LTPSs, in other words, to start producing country analogues of the LTPS, using it as a model for long term development plans. Within that context the LTPS is calling for a new generation of structural adjustment programs.

Clearly then the LTPS has crucial implications, not just for the welfare of

African people but also for the overall recovery and transformation process in Africa. As Africans we should subject it to systematic analysis and debate to try to assess the extent to which it complements or obstructs Africa's own indigenous efforts as represented by the LPA, AAF-SAP and other documents.

As regards the Fraser Report, many Africans, especially people outside OAU and ECA circles, do not know what it is. But it is a major policy document that, if adopted, could determine Africa's pattern and structure of trade for years to come. We have, therefore, an obligation to at least understand what it is saying, whether we agree with it or not. Happily, on our behalf, the OAU has already reacted to the Fraser Report. As you are aware, two members of the Fraser Committee, France and, I suspect, Nigeria, represented by General Obasanjo, refused to sign the report because they considered it so bad. In effect, the OAU declined to adopt it – I don't say rejected it, and proposed an alternative African common position on commodity problems. In the circumstances, we think that an organization like ours, committed to broad African concerns and enlightenment, should bring the Fraser Report to public attention so that African academics, policy makers, popular social groups, can debate it and at least be aware of the issues it addresses.

The same applies to the Uruguay Round of GATT. These negotiations should also be put in their proper international context as has been done in most other regions of the world, and systematic complaints raised against them. In particular, during The Other Economic Summit (the counter summit of the poor nations of the world to the G7 Summit) in Houston in July 1990, it was decided to reject the Uruguay Round .

African countries should also take part in the debate and understand the issues at stake, especially because the Uruguay Round of negotiations were conducted behind closed doors and we have legitimate reasons to fear closed door negotiations. Africa has always been at the receiving end of international policies which have collectively marginalized our region.

As a result of the conflict between Europe and the United States the Uruguay Round negotiations broke down. Had this not happened this workshop would have been a post-mortem, the deal would have been signed and we would be picking up the pieces and waiting for a response from our countries.

What would have been the effect upon Africa if agreement had been reached at the Uruguay Round?

1. Studies such as "Agricultural Development in the Third World in Relation to the Uruguay Round of GATT", made quantitative estimates of the

possible impact of the implementation of the Uruguay Round recommendations and concluded that , if agreement was reached, Africa would lose an average of $2-3 billion a year.

2. The development principle, recognised in the present GATT, would have been removed. This principle allows for "relative reciprocity", the technical basis for granting special concessions to developing countries in maintaining certain tariff levels and other non -trade measures to protect themselves.

3. A new organisation, the International Trade Organisation , was proposed which would threaten the sovereignty of Third World Countries. It would have had the power to enforce trans-border free trade in commodities, and non-border free trade in investment, banking, insurance and so on.

4. Foreign companies would have had the "right of establishment" in our countries, that is, they would have had to be treated as we treat our own indigenous companies. Programmes which prohibit foreign companies from operating in certain sectors of the economy, or which limit their ownership of equity shares in companies they set up to a certain percentage, would now be allowed.

5. Rules regulating Trade-Related Investment Measures (TRIMS) would have done away with local-content regulation. Multi-nationals could have come to an African country, brought all components and just assembled there, with less than 10% of value being added.

6. Technological exchanges between our countries and advanced countries would have been governed by Trade-Related Intellectual Property Rights (TRIPS). When a company from an advanced country introduced a technology into your country you would have had to grant it a patent over that technology, denying yourself access to it. This can already be done under GATT, but if TRIPS were established the monopoly would be almost total. In addition, in service areas like banking, insurance, travel and transport, it would no longer be possible to restrict the use of foreign-owned services.

7. On environmental concerns, existing checks and balances to control risks to health from certain products or activities would have been modified. There would be maximum standards instead of minimum standards. An individual country would not be able to refuse commodities because they did not meet minimum safety standards. The International Trade Organisation would pronounce on maximum standards.

This workshop is intended to initiate systematic debates on the World Bank's LTPS , and to broaden Africa's critique of the Fraser Report and the

Uruguay Round. The workshop is designed to involve policy makers and academics as well as a cross section of African workers, women, youth and peasants who will be most intimately affected by these documents and policies.

In particular, the workshop aims to break Africa's intellectual silence about the World Bank's LTPS. It was launched with fanfare and it is about time that the internal revolution and debate over it gathered momentum. We must not allow the policy perscriptions of the LTPS to be forced on our people by default because we did not speak out or complain.

The disasterous failure of ongoing orthodox SAPs and the proposal for new generation SAPs in the LTPS demand a systematic and vigorous evaluation of this document. This workshop is also designed to provide intellectual and broad popular support to the patriotic work of the ECA and the OAU in defending the integrity of African interests against the rapacious machinations of Africa's exploiters.

For some time we have been disturbed by the suggestions of the Bretton Woods institutions and their allies that it is only the ECA and the OAU that misguidedly oppose their programs. This implies that otherwise their programs and policies are acceptable and welcomed by the majority of Africans. This of course is not true. Since the 1980s the majority of Africans in their various locations have been mounting sustained resistance to the policies and programs of the IMF and World Bank, whether stabilization or social adjustment programs. It is in the context of that opposition that the expression "IMF Riots" has become almost a household phrase across Africa.

The wealthy industralized countries are trying through the World Bank and IMF, and increasingly through an overpowering and all-regulating new GATT agreement, to extend and tighten their control of the world economy in general as well as the national economies of developing countries, all African countries included. This would amount to nothing less than the recolonization of Africa.

The Institute for African Alternatives (IFAA), at this critical juncture, organised this important workshop to respond to these documents and policies that are being foisted on African countries. Addis Ababa was chosen as the venue as it is the headquarters of the OAU and ECA, which have already contributed so much to exposing the causes of the continent's crisis and postulating alternative policy perscriptions.

We hoped the workshop would be attended not only by policy makers from the ECA and OAU but from other African countries too. It was designed to broaden the debate and raise awareness of these policies because we firmly believe that a major reason many unpopular and inapropriate policies and programs are foisted on African countries is that our people are not even aware of these policies or the damage they do.

Our Institute feels that we should change this, in that as far as possible whenever policies are formulatted which have a direct bearing on African countries they should immediately be made into political documents. We say that advisedly. Even the United Nations system is increasingly becoming aware that its development and other documents are not being implemented because of this failure to make them into political documents in the sense that they are disseminated and distributed very widely, not only to government ministers and embassies but also to ordinary Africans in universities, research institutes, trade union organizations, women's groups, youth organizations, peasant groups and in all other locations.

This is the surest way of ensuring that we will be able to mobilize the generality of our population in support of policies in their interests. It is only when people can see their interests reflected fully in publications and documents that it will be possible to mobilize their energies on a sustained basis to implement such policies and programs.

In addition, only if our people, in their diverse social forces, can see the evil effects, and the negative impact of many of these foreign -inspired policies on their welfare and the progress of their countries will it be possible for them to give the kind of political support to African governments and to our Pan-African institutions, which they need, in opposing these policies. African countries learned a bitter lesson in the 1980s, namely that, when structural or orthodox restructural programs were being implemented in most African countries the generality of our people were not even aware of them. There was thus no question of the people supporting their governments or opposing what they did not know about.

We think we must correct that situation. At all times our Institute, along with other organizations, will give systematic support not only to our Pan-African institutions but to ordinary Africans in order to bring them to understand the deeper meanings and implications of all major policies and programs that affect their lives. This is the job of the "Interpreter"; our Institute is a body of interpreters. We stand between the major international organizations and the Pan-African organizations like the OAU, ECA , the African Development Bank and the generality of Africans, as women, as students and so on. So, when we hear of major policies and documents affecting our people we will have the responsibility of interpreting them, making them available to our people in the remotest corners of Africa. This is why we are a grassroots organization and it is one of our major functions to ensure that major policy documents and programs are known to our people. We help to demystify them by interpreting these policies and documents in simple language that our people can understand.

We think that this is fully in line with the implementation, which we think is urgent, of the African Charter for Popular Participation in Development. If that Charter is to have meaning it must ensure that documents and policies like the LTPS, the Fraser Report, Uruguay Round of GATT are made accessible to the generality of Africans so that our people in their various locations are able to participate in the debates over policy options .

One of the major constraints to the effective transformation and development of African countries is the lack of effective popular participation. There are two issues here. One is that if development means the mobilization of the resources of our people you cannot develop unless you persuade the people that their interests are involved in what you are doing. In most cases, even at the level of development plans in our countries, these are announced over television but the people don't see how their interests, their jobs, the schooling for their children, their health care are reflected in these documents and so they ignore them. As a result our governments are not able to mobilize our populations to implement these policies and programs, and this is why, year in year out, many of our policies and programs fail.

We feel that the 1990s are favorable for relaunching the process of recovery and transformation of Africa by revising that situation and trend.

The second major reason why we think this involvement and direct participation of our people should be encouraged at this point is the fact that all too often the impression is being given that we Africans are indifferent. That whatever is not forbidden is allowed and in fact, in many of our campaigns against debt and SAP in Europe, people ask us:

"What are your people saying about these things?"and we say, "Well, our people have been demonstrating, they are dying in riots and so on." But in many cases the Western media suppresses much of this information. Where they don't, they say , "Well it's the result of tribal hostility, because Africans can only act and interact at the level of tribe, not at the level of principles." We have to eliminate that kind of argument and the best way of doing so is to engage in this type of activity.

I was talking to some friends in an international conference recently and they told me, "You know what? Many of the policies and programs that the IMF, World Bank, and these international organizations impose on Africa, they don't dare to apply to Asia or Latin America."

We intend to change that. It is one of our avowed objectives and I promise you that we will discharge that commitment on behalf of all of us.

PART ONE
"Sub-Saharan Africa: from Crisis to Sustainable growth"

INDUSTRIAL DEVELOPMENT STRATEGIES

Khetso Gordham

The changes taking place in the world have changed the socio-economic and political context we live in. In South Africa, one of the many implications of these changes has been, I think, greater emphasis on the need to recognise specific of conditions affecting a particular country and the need for greater flexibility in policy options. This comes from a growing recognition that ideology-determined analysis and policies do not necessarily reflect the real balance of forces on the ground or the realistic way forward. This is reflected in the discussion on the question of nationalisation in South Africa. While the inherited wisdom of past socialist experiments suggests that nationalisation and state control are central policy measures, there is a call for a more creative search for policies that will be appropriate under current conditions. This is not to deny that there remain fundamental contradictions between different world views and class or social forces in society. Despite these contradictions, the changes have opened up some space for a more rigorous exchange of ideas and views, which has the potential of contributing to finding more creative answers to our problems.

The new emphasis poses a challenge to all engaged in the economic debate in developing countries, to find the most appropriate policy options to respond to the crisis. This requires some consensus about the causes and nature of the crisis, a common analysis of the existing reality and how we arrived at it and also some agreement on short and medium term objectives. This is difficult since varying class interests and world views will impact heavily on these questions. Therefore, the challenge in the debate is to deepen the consensus on fundamental issues to the greatest extent possible, making for more useful policy discussions.

The democratic forces in South Africa as elsewhere are disadvantaged because those that wield power, both economic and political, have a greater possibility of realising their policies. This does not reduce the importance of putting forward policies that represent the interests of the majority, or of developing strategies for struggle around these policy demands to allow for an eventual change in the balance of forces and for their realization.

It is within this perspective that I will make a limited critique of the industry section of the World Bank report on Sub-Saharan Africa, "From Crisis to Sustainable Growth".

OVERVIEW OF THE SECTION ON INDUSTRY

The report points to the poor performance of the manufactureing sector in SSA, which contributed only 10% to GDP and 9% to overall employment on average from 1965 to 1987. Whatever the debates might be, this statistic, we can all agree, is a cause of major concern.

The central reason advanced for this is 'too much government'. Some of the other explanations are: incorrect focus on physical capacity with an emphasis on heavy industry which resulted in 'unwise' public investment decisions not suited to local conditions; irrational protective and regulatory policies to promote import substitution which encouraged investment but did not result in innovation or competitiveness; and the lack of attention to human resource development together with the replacement of expatriates with inexperienced nationals.

While these factors might have contributed to the stagnation that characterised industrial performance from the seventies onwards, they fail to penetrate fully the reasons. The report fails to recognise that the World Bank and allied international financial institutions promoted import substitution industrialisation (ISI) policies in the 70s by lending indiscriminately and supporting capital intensive, heavy industrial projects, knowing that markets were protected. Nor does it incorporate into the analysis the open nature of these economies, which made them susceptible to changes in the world economy. Accordingly, it does not account for the impact of the international crisis of industry, which affected even the industrialised world, with its roots in the limitations of the 'fordist' mass production paradigm, which brought to the fore problems with the inefficient focus on scale, the inflexibility of single purpose machinery, constricting demand and under-utilisation.

The uniqueness of the SSA decline in industry and its inability to absorb the shocks during this international crisis need elaboration. Finally the report does not account for the role played by trans-national corporations (TNCs) whose power allowed them to invest without taking any responsibility for developing local capacity, or making technology agreements that would benefit the domestic economy while they maintained SSA as suppliers of primary goods that faced falling commodity prices.

RECOMMENDATIONS

The report notes that world trends in industry are moving away from competition based on price; hence cheap labour and economies of scale are becoming less important. The new emphasis is on competition based on innovation, product quality, flexible production techniques and product differentiation. This suggests that if Africa is to take advantage of these trends it will need to increase links with foreign partners and provide incentives to export. Industrial growth will need to be linked closely to the ability to raise agricultural incomes and benefit from increased demand, and also to incentives to agricultural producers to increase output.

More specifically it suggests:

1. Industry should be restructured towards high growth, competitive enterprises that are linked to domestic demand. This will require the removal of loss making enterprises and new investment. Industry should further seek to become competitive enough to penetrate export markets. Backward linkages to help the development of the intermediate and capital goods sectors should be developed.

2. The key to industrial growth is the movement away from central planning to a market oriented approach. Accordingly it calls for a changed role for government, less directing of industrialisation, increased privatisation of state industry, deregulation, reduction in protectionist policies, liberalisation of trade barriers and a market in foreign exchange (forex). Government should become a facilitator by providing infrastructure, building up the institutional and human resource base, providing incentives for investment, employment creation and ensuring that the legal and financial systems function well.

3. Market opportunities should be opened up. The domestic market could be expanded by providing for the lower income category. This could be done by promoting the informal sector and building up the 'missing' small and medium sized enterprises. A realistic

exchange rate (devaluation) would encourage the use of local supplies and deregulation would allow these enterprises a legal status to help them develop and compete with big industry. The key to competitiveness is rationalising protectionist policies so they no longer protect inefficient enterprises. Regional and overseas markets will be important in facilitating competition and technology transfers. Trade and forex liberalisation and foreign partnerships and sub-contracting will contribute to this process.

4. Industrial capabilities in relation to education and training should be developed, both at the formal level and on the job, and a more conscious policy adopted on developing science and technology capacity.

SOUTH AFRICA'S INDUSTRIAL DEVELOPMENT

The growth of the manufactureing sector was central to post-war development in South Africa. Manufacturing, which accounted for only 13% of GDP in 1946, accounted for 23% in 1978. When the economy went into decline in the mid 70s, manufacturing slowed down, even relative to the rest of the economy. There has been a fall of 1.7% per annum in per capita incomes since 1981. Indicators of the crisis include an unemployment figure of 3.5 million and a Gene co-efficient measure of 0.7, making it a country with one of the most unequal income distributions in the world, where the top 5% own 88% of all personal wealth.

Manufacturing grew in the 50s and 60s as a result of major inflows of capital, the governments tariff protection policy significant investment by the state, stable forex earning from gold and relatively cheap labour.

The reasons for the decline of the manufacturing sector and the economy as a whole can be traced to structural problems of the growth path and the nature of the manufacturing sector.

The ISI model was based on using expensive imports to cater for the very limited white market resulting in very inefficient production of consumer goods. The majority were excluded from any meaningful role in the economy, even from jobs in the skilled sectors. This had serious implications for a growing industrialised economy.

Although there was a consistent emphasis on ISI, the South Africa economy remained heavily dependent on imports. Since the 1920s the ratio of imports to GDP has remained at 24%. It remained so in the 1980s. Even today 50% of machinery is imported.

Failure to increase manufactured exports has not helped. Despite the growth, manufactured exports represent only 10% of total exports. Over 50% of this is accounted for by basic metals. The inefficient ISI model, the high cost of many inputs as a result of protection, the relative increase in wages, the collapse of the Bretton Woods system and the subsequent instability of forex earnings and political factors such as sanctions have all contributed to this.

The highly capital intensive nature of industry has affected both growth and employment in the manufacturing sector. While capital stock per worker went up from 2.6% in 1955-60 to 5.9% in 1980-85, productivity increased only 2% per annum, resulting in an overall decrease of 30% in the productivity of capital.

The response to the decline of manufacturing has been a growing focus on rationalisation, mergers and speculative activity, with the result that fixed productive investment has fallen. In 1986, fixed investment represented only 40% of the 1980 figure.

Despite the many differences between SSA and South African industry, there are many common problems. With a bit of oversimplification, three strategies can be identified in the debate about how best to develop industry in the future. The first is the neo-liberal, export orientation path, which calls for the restructuring of the manufacturing sector so that it becomes competitive and can penetrate export markets. This extends into a move which decreases the role of the state, encourages privatisation, and provides the necessary tax and related incentives to attract the private sector. The emphasis is on the export of beneficiated minerals, thereby attempting to resuscitate the old capital intensive, primary goods model. This model would benefit capital, those employed in those sectors and would have minimum impact on the majority. This falls into line with the World Bank's proposals.

The second and third development strategies are variations of the 'inward industrialisation model'. The free-market, conservative variant equates inward industrialisation with deregulation which would result in rapid growth of informal and small enterprises in response to growing urbanisation. This is similar to what the report recommends. The 'left' variation sees inward industrialiasation as part of investment in a way which would result in the creation of an expanded mass market. A crucial aspect of this strategy is state intervention in directing investments towards labour intensive production of basic goods.

This background on South African industrial development will serve as a reference point in my attempt to present a limited critique of the LTPS's report's recommendations.

COMMENTS ON THE RECOMMENDATIONS OF THE WORLD BANK

The track record of the World Bank is well documented elsewhere, so I do not propose to delve into that, but, I think it is important not to produce a knee jerk response to ideas because they emanate from a particular ideological position. It is most useful to consider them in the light of the weak position of industrial development within generally crisis-ridden economies and the objective of securing economic growth that has redistribution to the poor as one of its main aims.

I find many of the ideas contained in the report useful. It correctly identifies the problems of overvalued exchange rates, unproductive protectionary measures, an ISI model that focuses on a limited, rich market, the absence of small and medium sized enterprises and inefficient state bureaucracies. And many of its recommendations on future strategy are in general terms unobjectionable. Here I refer to the need to raise agricultural incomes to provide increased demand, the need to explore markets at domestic, regional and international level, with the aim of increasing competitive ness, technology transfer and enhancing the possibility of moving into the intermediate and capital goods sector, the need to invest in high growth industries that are linked to the domestic market and equally to emphasise the development of human resources and a stronger institutional framework.

There are however many limitations and weaknesses:

1. The report is strong on generalities but very weak on substantive details. It is consistently vague about its proposals. It talks about restructuring towards high growth but says nothing about what these are and how this growth can be achieved. It does not spell out the consequences of following its recommendations, which at best represent a shopping list of ideas that are at times contradictory and would be difficult to put into a feasible development strategy.
2. Its insistence on emasculating the state is worrying. Whilst it calls for

the state to move towards playing a facilitative role, it continues to suggest the need for a process of directed restructuring and the conscious development of small and medium enterprises. All this requires consensus building within the economy. The question is, who will take responsibility for this and who is best placed to do so if not the state ? It has been fairly conclusively shown that the state played a central role in the NIC's industrial strategy. As put by Gordon White, "... in Japan, South Korea and Taiwan, among the most dramatic and equitable cases in the history of capitalist development, industrialisation has in each case been accompanied by agressive state intervention." The authorities have acted to guide markets and modulate the competitive process in a way that neo-classical economists say public officials cannot get right. The report's continued use of the NIC's as champions of the free market approach, a now discredited or at least questionable myth, is unhelpful. This issue is central to the debate unfolding in South Africa. The ANC is convinced that without strategic state intervention in industry, in making and directing investment and regulating private industry, we will be reproducing the existing levels of inequality. We are convinced that sustainable growth is linked to the creation of a changed pattern of effective demand for basic goods, which must be accompanied by income and investment redistribution in favour of the marginalised millions, and that this will not be achieved by free market mechanisms. While accepting the need to find export markets, it is clear that the absence of state intervention and a conscious technology policy which targets industries and concentrates research and development efforts has contributed to the failure of exports and the development of a capital goods sector in South Africa.

While much work remains to be done in identifying sectors that should be targeted, we remain committed to the state playing a central role in this process. Further, the ANC supports the formation of a national science and technology policy council which will involve industrialists, trade unions and academics, to develop policy in this area.

3. While the need to export is clear, the report does not give adequate consideration to the 'export pessimism' which has, I think, some validity for Africa. The consolidation of the Pacific Rim, Europe and North American trade areas, the rise of new protectionism and related non-tariff barriers raise serious constraints for exports from Africa. The

development of micro-electronics can undermine the low wage cost comparative advantage of the developing countries. Even the processing of raw materials is problematic. It faces the protectionist policies of the industrialised world and would require further capital intensive and probably import intensive investment. While the report overcomes the false dichotomy between domestic and export oriented industry and calls for an integrated approach, it does little to suggest how this can be done. Its suggestions on regional trade are useful certainly for Southern Africa in a post-Apartheid context.

4. The report fails to point out the limitations of its inward industrialisation, upgrading the informal sector proposal. While deregulation could lead to heightened activity in this sector, from a labour point of view it carries with it the possibility of the emergence of low wage sweat shops. The absence of an internal dynamism in the informal sector, makes it reliant for growth on the formal sector. Finally the report does not point to the need for inward industrialisation to be accompanied by a conscious policy of redistribution, or we would simply be engaging in Keynesian demand expansion which would not change the pattern of effective demand and would be inflationary ?

   The ANC has put forward as a policy of option a version of inward industrialisation within the framework of growth through redistribution. We believe that through the budget, prescribed assets and related mechanisms we could initiate, for example, major public works programmes to produce low cost housing. This would generate employment, provide for basic needs and form an important part of the engine of growth based on redistribution. The central challenge is to find an industrial development model that integrates both non-capital and import intensive industry and is redistributive.

5. The question of ownership and control of the industrial sector is not addressed. This becomes crucial when we look at the policy of privatisation proposed by the report. The obvious danger is that the only groups that can afford to buy are the already powerful corporations, which will lead to further concentration. This is particularly true for South Africa, where four major conglomerates control 81% of the share capital and dominate the capital markets. They would be the only real contenders in any privatisation. The need for more creative forms of

ownership and control other than state or private is not explored. Co-operative, social and worker ownership and control are options being investigated by the ANC, which also supports the idea of small and medium sized enterprises which facilitate employment creation and democratic control. The report does not accord any role to labour in the process of industrial development or restructuring. The ANC sees a crucial role for workers in the economy through independent trade unions. Already some of the workers are beginning to contribute to industrial restructuring plans. This needs to be extended into a role for organised labour in investment planning, developing a democratic industrial relations framework, defining training needs and procedures, intervening in determining work organisation and in control over collective capital formation schemes.

SMALL SCALE INDUSTRIES AND THE INFORMAL SECTOR IN TANZANIA

Bertha Koda

I. INTRODUCTION

In the forward to the LTPS Report the President of the World Bank implies that Africans cannot solve their socio-economic (and indeed political) problems without an external push. He suggests the need to consolidate cooperation between developed (DCs) and less-developed countries (LDCs) as partners in development. In fact the World Bank consistently advocates privatization and so-called partnership between North and South and underrates South-South relationships.

The LTPS Report makes the following assumptions:

1. That all African governments are problematic,
2. That LDCs and DCs can become equal partners in development
3. That greater cooperation between DCs and LDCs will ensure sustainable development
4. That increased aid will eventually lead to reduced dependency on aid
5. That local policies are the major factor contributing to the crisis in sub-Saharan Africa

Using the experiences of small scale industries in Tanzania, this paper proposes to show that DCs and LDCs have never been equal partners and are not likely to be, that cooperation between DCs and LDCs will not ensure sustainable development and that there is a dialectical relationship between aid and increased dependency.

II. ENTREPRENEURSHIP AND THE INFORMAL SECTOR

The LTPS maintains that there is no shortage of entrepreneurship in Africa. Indeed early explorers who came into contact with traditional craftsmen and women, blacksmiths etc., compared these village units with the small industrial centres of pre-industrial Germany. Iron-ore works were noticed in almost every region of Tanzania. Of course the rate of technological development was determined by the limited consumption and productive needs of the people.

When the colonialists came with their cash and market economy, they systematically robbed local, traditional small scale industries of their initiatives and subjugated them. However, after Independence, the sector popularly known as the informal sector revived and increased its contribution to GNP in most African countries . This sector gained statistical recognition in 1970, thanks to the ILO sponsored Employment Strategy Mission to Kenya which highlighted its labour absorption capacity. Thereafter, similar studies in almost every African country have enriched the understanding of both the structure and functioning of the sector.

The informal sector, which includes small scale industries and commercial units, tends to be the most dynamic part of most African economies in employment generation and the provision of basic needs in the cheapest possible way. This sector is also important in combating the problems associated with inequality and poverty. However, both national and sectoral policies have tended to discriminate against it.

During the next three decades the population of sub-Saharan Africa is expected to grow by at least 600 million people. Entrepreneurs will be expected to create more jobs. But the numbers of business-minded Africans is limited for historical reasons. Under colonialism Africans could not accumulate capital since all the surplus was appropriated and repatriated by the colonialists. These same masters encouraged Asians rather than Africans to establish business enterprises in parts of Africa, e.g. East Africa, thus monopolising the business sector. The capacity for Africans to accumulate capital was further reduced as economic conditions deteriorated. Low prices for primary products in the 1980s aggrevated this problem and private African capital investment in business remains weak.

However, the informal sector is not doing too badly. It actually gained momentum during the 1970s when demand for its products grew dramatically due to the shortage of inputs for local industry as a result of shortage of foreign exchange. In some countries governments adopted policies to boost the informal sector. Cooperative, private, family and partnership arrangements were encouraged. Other factors leading to its expansion in Tanzania, for instance, included the fall in real wages, price increases, the diminishing ability of agriculture to sustain rural people, etc. Virtually everybody was forced to search for an income-generating activity. An increasing number of women and children could be found doing all sorts of jobs to earn a living or supplement the incomes of other family members.

Recognition of the importance of this sector in national statistics increasingly gained ground. According to ILO estimates it accounts for 60% of the sub-Saharan urban labour force with an average output of US$15 million in 17 African countries or 20% of GNP (South, 1990:12-13 as quoted by Maganya,E."The Role of the Association of Tanzania Employers in the Informal Sector", unpublished report, 1990). In Tanzania this sector's contribution increased from 9.8% of GNP in 1970 to 31.4% in 1978 (Malyamkono and Bagachwa "The Second Economy in Tanzania" 1990:147).

There are a wide range of informal industrial and business activities. The entrepreneurs are also of diverse backgrounds - part-timers, full-timers, workers, migrants, fresh school leavers and people "redeployed" from the public sector.

One important feature is the clearly defined gender roles. Women tend to concentrate in areas compatible with their reproductive roles, particularly childcare. Womens informal sector activities are therefore often extensions of domestic responsibilities. They also concentrate in areas with less growth potential and which require little outlay. Petty trade, selling cooked foods, beer brewing and selling are a few examples.

Some activities, such as prostitution, are age specific and young women tend to be predominant. These tend to be better paid than those in which older women are predominant, such as vegetable selling. In the market place, while men and women may be active, women usually sell vegetables and cheap commodities while men sell goods such as fish with a higher rate of return. Indeed, female-dominated productive activities tend to require little capital and skill and to provide low returns and little stability.

The success of new enterprises and their capacity to expand depends on information and knowledge of the trade. Women usually have no access to this. Their knowledge is usually compartmentalized. They have no great capacity to recruit labour since they seldom make decisions related to resource control and allocation. Differential distribution of authority in the household is a great limitation.

The small-scale nature of most enterprises in the informal sector is partly due to financial constraints. Most are not considered credit-worthy. Studies done in Tanzania and elsewhere in Africa show that 87% of all capital for micro enterprises is raised in the family with 10% loaned by relatives and only 3% from formal banks or government grants.

The limited role of the formal financial market in the development of the informal sector emanates both from the insufficient capacity of this sector to absorb funds and its inability to meet the lending criteria.

The problems of financing micro-enterprises are not confined to lack of funds. Bureaucracy and corruption within the banks are grave problems. Female entrepreneurs tend to be more adversely affected due to their lack of information and because the bureaucrats, who have the final say in approving loans, are usually men and tend to distance themselves from women.

III. THE WORLD BANK'S "PARTNERSHIP" APPROACH

The "partnership" strategy for European and African entrepreneurs propounded by the World Bank is not new. The Tanzanian government has long experience of joint ventures with foreign capital. Our experience has shown that even when the local share is more than 50% , foreign partners have used a series of mechanisms to extract huge but indirect profits for remittance abroad. Joint ventures are usually "turn-key" projects with expensive equipment and managerial needs. Even where contracts include a component for training local personnel, the experience has been discouraging. An increasing number of expatriates are coming from European countries and, in Mtwara, for instance, they hold all the top positions in sectoral projects.

An alternative form of partnership tried by SIDO, the Sister Industry Programme, has also proved unsuccessful. It involved the Swedish International Development Administration (SIDA) providing investment and Swedish companies providing technical and managerial training. Three ventures at a cost of T.shs.185 million and employing 1,067 people, were established between 1976 and 1987.

Their performance has been no better than other joint enterprises. These units operate below capacity because they have not managed to escape the dependency syndrome. They have been dependent on imports of raw materials, machinery and spare parts, the very problem the program was designed to avoid. Only two of the nine units were designed to use local raw materials, and choice of products tended to dictate not only the choice of technology and raw materials but also the mode of transferring technology (Sverker, 1981, p.8).

The Tanzanian experience of "partnership" is that the state controls neither the labour processes nor the manoeuvres of foreign capital; that domestic accumulation is restricted and technological dependence perpetuated. The World Bank's proposal for partnership between North and South is therefore not the answer to economic development.

FUNDING SUSTAINABLE DEVELOPMENT IN SUB-SAHARAN AFRICA (SSA)

Wilfred W. Asombang

The purpose of this brief paper is (i) to comment on Chapter 8 of the World Bank's study and appraise the development funding prescriptions it propounds, and (ii) to introduce an alternative partnership and social system approach to the funding of development and tranformation in SSA.

MISPLACED CRITICISM OF THE "FIRST GENERATION OF AFRICAN LEADERS"

The Bank seems to attribute post-independence policy distortions to the "first generation of African leaders" who "adopted economic strategies that echoed the ideas of prominent economists of the day" (p.16). Yet is it not common knowledge that the former colonialists were determined to perpetuate the ruthless exploitation of independent African countries? Is it not also true that the formulation of the first post-independence development plans was undertaken by British, French and IMF/World Bank economists who transplanted orthodox theories and models to sustain Africa's continued dependence on the factories and markets of Europe and North America ?

The unsuspecting "first generation of African leaders" had just emerged from many years of callous colonization and were preoccupied with the social rehabilitation of the population and nation-building. They counted on economists from the erstwhile colonial countries and the World Bank to provide objective assistance in planning and programming socio-economic development efforts. Little did they realize that the real intentions of colonial economists were to safeguard the short and long-term economic interests of European countries.

The Bank's persistent criticism of African leaders and scholars must therefore be properly placed in the perspective of the legacy of colonial economic policy in independent African countries.

FORCING EMPIRICAL EVIDENCE TO FIT ORTHODOX THEORY

Investment prescriptions propounded in Chapter 8 of the LTPS reaffirm the resilience of the World Bank in the use of orthodox theories as a basis for the formulation of the conditionality of SAPs.

The "Development expenditure", and "Reorienting investment" sections of Chapter 8 (pp 163/4) state the following:

> "East Asian countries, which grew fastest, had investment rates averaging about 25 to 30 per cent".
>
> "Yet, despite high average investment rates in Mauritania (30 per cent) and Togo (24 per cent), the average growth rates were quite low".
>
> "The future development strategy aims to raise the efficiency of investment... the rate of investment, both public and private, would have to be about 25 per cent of GDP to attain a growth rate of 5 per cent a year".

Notwithstanding the empirical evidence from Mauritania and Togo cited by the Bank, it regards the correlation between rate of investment and average rate of growth of output as universally sacrosanct. Instead of breaking new ground and finding out why this orthodox theory of investment-GDP ratio (capital/output ratio) does not seem to give expected outcomes in African countries, the Bank insists on arguing for the continued application of investment theories that have a proven record of failure.

It is difficult to believe that the World Bank is not aware of the history of economic thought and empirical evidence on invesment ratios and rate of growth in industialized and other countries. Way back in 1951 a United Nations report on "Measures for the Economic Development of Underdeveloped Countries" asserted, among other things, that annual expenditure of one per cent of national income, on research and extension, plus 3 per cent on capital on and off farms would increase output in underdeveloped countries by 2.5 per cent a year, equivalent to an increase of one per cent in national income per year. After 40 years of trial-and-error and failure, the World Bank (p.164) still advocates that: "For the agriculture sector as a whole, including rural infrastructure, an investment of 4 per cent of GDP would be needed to achieve an annual growth rate of 4 per cent". In effect, according to World Bank logic, there is a one-to-one relationship between investment in the agriculture sector and the annual rate of growth! In manufacturing an investment of 3 per cent of GDP would achieve a yearly growth rate of 5 per cent! Similar relationships have not been extended to human resource development and other sectors perhaps because the authors of the Bank's investment-GDP correlation argument are remorsefully aware of the unrealistic application of neo-orthodox theory as recently as 1989!

The investment criteria advocated by the World Bank are flawed in many ways which have been adequately documented* and demonstrated in practice in various countries. The Bank apparently uses some undefined rule-of-thumb to protect the growth rates expected from some hat-trick investment figure!

Despite the Bank's assertion that the composition of investment should reflect priorities on developing human resources and creating an enabling environment (p.163), there is no investment proportionality established between GDP and employment generation. The problems of intra-sectoral complementarities and sectoral linkages as well as the mutual relationships of sectoral externalities do not feature in the Bank's investment criteria. This disarticulation of investment and growth runs through the whole of Chapter 8.

The Bank has not convinced its clientele that there is a determinate functional relationship between the rate of investment and the rate of growth of GDP either in theory or in practical applications.

** See for instance, Centre for International Studies, Massachusetts Institute of Technology, Investment Criteria and Economic Growth (Asia Publishing House Bombay, 1961).*

CONTRADICTIONS BETWEEN ANALYSIS AND PRESCRIPTION

In the section "Mobilizing Domestic Resources" (p.164), the Bank argues that Africa's declining returns on investments and consequent problems in mobilizing domestic resources is not due to drought nor to "falling world demand" for Africa's exports. According to the Bank: "everything points to declining productivity". It is contradictory to expect productivity to increase in the face of drought and falling world demand for Africa's commodities. It should interest the Bank to know that African farmers reactions to falling demand for their commodities have included the cutting down of cocoa and coffee trees in some countries and the substitution of food crops that have a ready local market.

For once, the Bank admits (p.27) that "half of the completed rural development projects financed by the World Bank in Africa had failed". This amounts to the participation of the Bank in the leakages of domestic resources from rural Africa.

The argument that "consumption taxes are preferable because they do not adversely affect production" is untenable. Similarly, the over-generalization that "commodity taxes do not cascade through the production process" (p.165) is puzzling. The mix-up of consumption taxes and taxes on production gives the impression that there is no relationship between consumption and production, that is between demand and supply. One wonders what type of resource mobilization policy could emerge from the Bank's prescription that "resource mobilzation and development would be better served by a gradual shift from taxes on trade towards taxes on consumption and income". The apparent confusion in taxation concepts is intriguing. Issues such as tax base, taxable capacity, tax effort, trends toward value added tax (VAT) and programmes to improve the capabilities of Africa's productive forces are not emphasized in relation to domestic resource mobilization

There are few people who would disagree, in principle, on the need for user charges. The problem of cost-recovery is not that of " improving metering, billing, and accountablility" as argued by the Bank (p.166) but of training an army of technicians and artisans to improve the quality and maintenance of services at all times. Availability of technical skills in services such as water and sewarage, electricity, telecommunications, roads and drainage could reduce the cost of these services through improvements in efficiency. It is common knowledge that in both British and French colonial regimes in Africa there was a general disdain for the promotion of technical education, resulting in the post-independence shortage of technical skills to maintain basic services. It is not surprising therefore, to find expatriate technicians from Europe employed to maintain cargo conveyor belts or air-conditioning equipment at airports under projects financed from foreign loans. The statement (p.166) that "public finance analysts have paid little attention to the private sector's willingess to pay for social services" does not reflect the concern of public finance analysts.

The Bank, in one breath, applauds Botswana's prudent control of public expenditure and management of commodity booms and bursts (p.167) and at the same time acquiesces to the country's reliance on the mining sector which has few linkages with the rest of the economy. That Botswana has an exceptional record of political stability is not in doubt. However, the non-renewable nature of the diamond and other mineral resources, the special financial and economic relationship with South Africa and extreme income disparity in the midst of plenty are issues which the Bank should not eclipse because the government itself has highlighted them in order to take corrective developmental action.

The Burkina Faso case study on "cost-saving procurement of petroleum products" by a state-owned company, Societe Nationale des Hydrocarbons de Burkina (SONABHY) (p.168), is an example of a success story of a public enterprise that demonstrated the feasibility of prudent public expenditure control. Bank lending regulations on sourcing of imports would have insisted on procurement only from member countries even if cheaper sources in non-member countries were available. This case study should discourage generalizations on the inefficiency or mismanagement of public enterprises and underline the need for a balanced view of the status of public and private sector enterprises in Africa's development.

THE ROLE OF EXTERNAL RESOURCES IN THE DEVELOPMENT EQUATION

This report reorchestrates the 1970s orthodox advice to African countries. The Bank argues that increased exports are conducive to the rapid growth of African economies. Empirical evidence** suggests, however, that there is little relationship between the degree of export orientation and the rate of economic growth in poor countries. Growth is more likely to be affected by export performance after a country has achieved some minimum level of socio-economic development. The letter and spirit of the Berg Report are echoed in the LTPS. African countries are in essence required to unilaterally reduce barriers to imports, liberalize and open up their economies, increase incentives for exporters and eliminate agricultural subsidies. Needless to say, this is one of the standard recipes of SAPs. Now 30 frustrating years of outward looking socio-economic development efforts call for urgent studies on inward looking development alternatives for the 1990s and beyond.

While the self-reliant philosophy of the Lagos Plan of Action (LPA) envisaged minimizing external resources in the development equation, the IMF and the IBRD seem to be initiating parallel concessional loan facilities to address the debt predicament on condition that the countries concerned have a donor-endorsed economic reform programme. While the World Bank launched the three-year Special Programme of Assistance (SPA) for low-income, debt-distressed SSA countries at the end of 1987, the IMF followed suit in 1988 by establishing the Enhanced Structural Adjustment Facility (ESAF). African countries, in the desperate position of "lender of last resort", are torn between the SPA and ESAF conditionality. Would a merger of the IMF and the IBRD not bring about economies of scale and relieve some of the pressures of SAPs ?

*** See, for instance, G K Helleiner, "Outward Orientation, Import Instability and Economic Growth; an Empirical Investigation" in Sanjaya Lal and Frances Stewart (eds.), Theory and Reality in Development (London, Mac-Millan Press, 1986) p.139.*

The Bank's caution on technical assistance is well placed and should be heeded by African governments and institutions (p.181). It is pointed out that "despite the education and training of a generation of Africans in economics, ministers of finance and plannning still choose expatriates to undertake policy analysis. Many governments lack confidence in local specialists and yield to the offers of expatriates often at little cost". The question is: what is the contribution of the IMF and IBRD to this state of affairs especially in situations where the position of local specialists is at variance with that of the IMF/IBRD alliance ?

A SOCIAL SYSTEM APPROACH TO FUNDING SUSTAINABLE DEVELOPMENT

There is apparent consensus between the World Bank and SSA countries that the 1980s was the lost decade for Africa, a decade of falling per capita incomes and accelerating ecological and human degradation. However, there is no consensus on practical measures to bring about a turnaround in Africa's socio-economic decline.

It is not obvious from Chapter 8 that the World Bank is ready to back away from its orthodox treatment of Africa's development, notwithstanding platitudes such as "Governments and donors alike must be prepared to change their thinking fundamentally in order to revive Africa's fortunes", "Africa's future can only be decided by Africans", and "respect for African values". The orthodox prescriptions on the reorientation of development expenditure in

Chapter 8 do not reflect the expected translation of platitudes into pragmatic action.

On the part of African countries, the need to consider development as an integrated social process has been underlined at several fora. The lessons for Africa's economic performance in the 1990s could be drawn from social, economic andpolitical factors which are multifaceted, endogenous and exogenous. These crucial lessons include the knowledge that:

(a) It is imprudent to attempt to address short-term problems to the detriment of long-term development goals;

(b) The persistent outward orientation of African economies tends to exacerbate the dependency syndrome and perpetuate underdevelopment;

(c) Failure to make the most efficient use of limited resources and reduce to the barest minimum wasteful and unproductive investment, as well as poor economic management, will undermine all economic development efforts;

(d) In African development priorities there should be no place for military hardware loans which industrialized countries are prepared to give for the asking, the focus should be on loans for productive investment including investment in human resources;

(e) The trend towards the marginalization of people from the development process must be reversed;

(f) The outflow of capital and human resources from Africa to the already industrialized countries must be arrested and reversed;

(g) Disillusionment with the development strategies of the past decade, the imminent establishment of a fully integrated European Community in 1992 and other regional economic blocs must impel African countries to speed up regionalism and economic integration to avert economic collapse;

(h) For Africa to succeed in the development and transformation of its productive forces, the forging of new partnerships is imperative: there must be new partnerships between African governments and the people; among African governments thermselves; and between Africa and its development partners. New partnerships imply that all partners should share in the losses as well as the benefits of development. The current outflow of resources to the World Bank and other finaciers does not reflect a partnership relationship as envisaged in the African development alternative.

The funding of development as a social system requires the abandonment of what Paul Streeten aptly describes as single-barrier theories of development such as the investment/GDP prescriptions in the LTPS. Development variables are causally interrelated and all conditions that constitue the quality of human life should be regarded as fundamental. In funding agriculture, for instance, the package of conditions which should be addressed in an integrated milieu must include output and incomes; production conditions; living conditions and levels of farmers; attitudes to work and life; institutions; and the multidimensional facets of policies.

STRUCTURAL ADJUSTMENT AND THE NIGERIAN RAILWAYS

Dr. L. A. Osunde

Between 1983 and 1985 more than 2,000 railway workers were forced to resign or take compulsory retirement as a result of the IMF. There was no pension for those who retired. Recently there was a plan to retrench over 2,000 more railway workers. The Union (NUR) set up a commission to look into the matter and warned the Government that if this happened they would close down the railway.

I should like to quote from the LTPS report to illustrate the position of the World Bank with regard to the railways:

> "Sub-Saharan African railway traffic has been declining both in absolute terms and in traffic shares. Ghana railway carried about 2.6 million tons of freight in the early 1970s and only 0.4 million tons by the mid 1980s. Nigerian railways lost 33% of its traffic from 1979 to 1986. In Sudan 40% of exports were carried by rail in 1980 but by 1986 the railway share had fallen to only 5%."

These are the facts but the question is, why is the railway declining and what are the costs ? Nobody has answered that question. The Nigerian railway was an income earning transport system before Independence. Then competition for the haulage of goods from the North and East to the South began. A number of road transport networks owned by Ministers and the Government emerged. As a result less and less money went into the railway until it ended up in debt. If this situation is rectified there is no reason why the Nigerian Railway System should not again become profit-making.

WHAT DOES THE WORLD BANK MEAN BY 'EMPOWERING ORDINARY PEOPLE'?

Ben Turok

It is now common talk that there is a crisis of self confidence inside the World Bank. This view is partly derived from the severe criticisms of the Bank by its former employees and partly by inference from its own publications. Of the former perhaps the most damning to emerge thus far are the comments of its former Vice President for Economic Development. Professor Stanley Fischer who attacked the "culture of secrecy" at the IMF and World Bank. He also criticised the Fund and Bank for operating in developing countries with "few checks and balances". He called for a "careful appraisal"of the Funds record, noting that there had been few serious evaluations recently. (FT 20.10.91)

Fischer's criticisms follow those of Percy Mistry, a former Finance Manager at the Bank, and Michael Irwin a former Vice President for Personnel and many others.

Even the Deputy Director of DG8 (Development Department) of the Commission of the European Community felt bound to say at a briefing for NGO's in London in 1991 that the World Bank had admitted substantial failures of structural adjustment and was working on a trial and error basis.

The press has been even more critical. A review of the World Development Report 1991 in the London Financial Times commented that "the report read like a teaching manual...one gets the impression the bank believes it has found the philosopher's stone of development economics...but it seems implausible that a single set of policies will suit all developing countries at all times." (FT July 8,1991)

More recently,Tony Hawkins wrote, "It would help if there were more willingness at the World Bank to acknowledge the failure of many of its

African policies.The recent claim that structural adjustment is working in Ghana, Togo and Tanzania is not supported by independent researchers,while numerous studies highlight the failure of reform programmes to revive investment, domestic as well as foreign." (FT October 14,1991)

Equally disconcerting are the occasional admissions by Bank officials that they are flying blind. Having cajoled most African countries to accept structural adjustment programmes,the head of the World Bank's Africa Bureau, Stephen Jaycox says,"Nobody knows what an effective Structural Adjustment Programme looks like. We cannot anticipate the adverse effects of Structural Adjustment policies." (Africa Update 1990)

The major 1989 World Bank study on Africa - SUB SAHARAN AFRICA: FROM CRISIS TO SUSTAINABLE GROWTH (LTPS) also fails to inspire confidence. The most positive statements it can manage are "SAPs are important steps in the right direction" (p62) and "Structural Adjustment Programmes are beginning to produce results, but only slowly."(p189). And yet what is at stake is not some minor aspect of policy but the very foundations of economic, social and political policy for the whole continent of Africa.

It is well known that stringent conditionalities ("harsh medicine" in IMF language) have been imposed on African governments. So how could Barber Conable, then President of the Bank say in the introduction to the LTPS report, "Africa's future can only be decided by Africans. External agencies can only play at most a supportive role." (p2). Indeed, government officials in Africa understand too well that toeing the World Bank line is a precondition for loans from the Bank and the International Monetary Fund. At the same time both these bodies know that their conditions can only be carried through by the very governments they excoriate so fiercely in their various reports.

A virtual campaign has been launched about " poor governance" in Africa, now the dominant explanation in the world press for the problems of the continent. While few would wish to deny the failures of government in Africa, the scale of the attack on governance goes beyond legitimate criticism. It smacks of a desire to distract from other causes of Africa's deterioration.

Firstly, there is the international dimension. The senior Vice President of the Bank, Maun Kureshi, has admitted that, "Nowhere has the external environment been so hostile to national efforts to restore growth as in Africa". Bank statistics in the LTPS report and elsewhere show that there was a net flow from Africa to the IMF and World Bank for the years 1986-1990, and that the terms of trade have moved drastically against Africa. The Bank has also conceded that developing countries will face a shortage of official development finance over the whole decade (F T 27.4.91).

Chief economist Lawrence Summers has said that since funds will be short, *"there had better be a lot of good ideas."* Whereas the Bank had transferred $9 per head from 1975 to 1980, in the period 1981-86 this figure would be $2 per head. Furthermore those countries not eligible to borrow soft loans would actually be transferring money to the Bank. Good governance is difficult in this international context.

Secondly, Bank criticism of African governance is designed to legitimate the private sector as against the state. The Report says "The private sector holds the key to future industrial growth." While the Bank cannot itself directly fund the private sector, free market policies are dominant in their approach. Presently, the US is pressing for the Bank to direct 50 per cent of its lending to the private sector by 1995 in return for an increase in funding to the International Finace Corporation, a Bank affiliate. The governance critique will then have paved the way for this change.

Thirdly, there is an attempt to substitute non-governmental organisations for government in development programmes.While there is indeed a much greater recognition of the important role of non-governmental agencies of all kinds, including churches, trade unions and the like, Bank efforts to reduce the role of government must be suspect. There are major areas of development which remain the province of government, especially as substantial local capital is lacking. (Recent findings are that SAPs fail crucially in encouraging local investment). The Report's apparent preference for grass-roots based NGO's as alternative structures seems merely to be an attempt to introduce new layers of monitoring and control which might serve non-people interests.

SPURIOUS CLAIMS ABOUT DEMOCRATISATION

What is the purpose of statements like, "people come first", and "the ultimate goal is to empower individuals and communities to take charge of their own development. The key is to strengthen local organisations." (Last chapter LTPS). Or, this statement from the foreword to LTPS:

> "The report sets out a range of proposals aimed at empowering ordinary people, especially women, to take greater responsibility for improving their lives, measures that foster grassroots organisation, that nurture rather than obstruct informal sector enterprises, that promote non-governmental and intermediary organisations. The growing conviction is

> that development must be more 'bottom up', less 'top down' and that a learning approach to programe design is to be preferred to the imposition of blue-prints."

We shall examine later on the claims about "bottom up" approaches, but it is rather extraordinary that the Bank should now propose a learning approach when it has imposed structural adjustment programmes as forcibly as the IMF, leading to serious deterioration right across the continent.

Bank economic diktat goes hand in hand with political conditionality. Has the Bank distanced itself from statements by members of the Paris Club such as was found in the Ethiopia Herald of 22 Jan 1991?

> "The French Finance Minister Berogovi told a news conference in New York on Monday, that the Paris Club had made progress towards cancelling large sums of debt owed by both Poland and Egypt. Poland needed special help because of its role in promoting democracy and free markets in Eastern Europe and Egypt because of the part it is playing in the US led alliance. (But) Western assistance to Cairo would still depend on Egypt signing an accord with the IMF."

There have been many cases of similar sticks and carrots being applied particularly in Eastern Europe and Africa.

When political conditionalities were first mooted in the press, there was much scepticism that international bodies like the Bank and the Fund, and Western governments for that matter, would exercise pressure so directly. Yet President Mitterand and Douglas Hurd publicly raised the proposition that "aid must be matched by better government". A USAID document endorsed this position suggesting that support for Nigerian projects should be contingent on the creation of democratic institutions.

Political conditionalities are often related to free market assumptions. "The connection between democratic practice is apparent...market systems need accountability, rule by law, and transparency in decision making." (OECD Development Assistance Committee Report 1990). Lann Walker, a US Ambassador, has argued that Nigerian projects should "support democratic institutions" more overtly. He also proposed a "democracy support fund"and an African Commission on Democratisation which would include non-Africans in its membership. We can speculate how Nigeria would react to such overtures.

Objectively, external pressure for democratisation, cannot be unhelpful for the continent, particularly as it reinforces the struggle for democracy by a broad range of social forces and the African masses across the continent. But Fund and Bank pressures come, strangely, from institutions which have for many years bolstered the most oppressive regimes in the Third World such as those of Mobutu, Moi, Rawlings and the like. Furthermore, these organisations wish to see the emergence of liberal democracies which will support their policies of liberalisation and freeing market forces which will open up Africa to Western multinationals. They will certainly not empower the African people, nor will a democratic development process flourish under liberalisation. State initiatives will be needed.

The reality is that new political conditionalities are not meant to reduce the power of Africa's elites, who bear so much responsibility for the wrong path taken since independence. Instead, they are designed to bring to power governments which will be even more pliable to Western pressure and more in tune with the aims of the new international order now being put into place by the G7.

These objectives were spelt out quite clearly at the G7 London Economic Summit on 17 July 1991.

> "We seek to build world partnership, based on common values,and to strengthen the international order. Our aim is to underpin democracy, human rights, the rule of law and sound economic management, which together provide the key to prosperity...we will promote a truly multilateral system...our shared objectives are a sustained recovery and price stability."

It is well understood that the G7 regards itself as the unofficial world government and that the IMF and World Bank take their direction from the G7. Yet this undemocratic, self selected, exclusive club claims to be, "underpinning democracy". Though it represents only 15% of the world's population it seeks to promote a "truly multilateral system". All its claims must be suspect in particular its "commitment" to "sustainable growth" and "new jobs" given its track record on forcing reductions in government spending and deflation and its resistance to reducing Third World debt. The amount owed by the South still exceeds the amount originally borrowed,notwithstanding massive payments on debt servicing.

Given the admitted "hostile international climate" particularly with respect to primary commodity prices and duties on imports from Africa , the G7 would do better to address the global inequalities they sustain and stop resisting all arguments for a fundamental reform of the systems of debt, trade, aid and land ownership (TOES Communique 17 July 1991).

It is rather surprising that the World Bank now stresses "empowerment" rather than the more common promptings for political pluralism, human rights and democratic opening. The reason appears to be a desire to open space for individual entrepreneurs, who are to be empowered over the state sector in the economy. The LTPS urges "a shift from central planning to a market-oriented approach, from regulation to competition." But this is also located in the context of structural adjustment which has nothing to do with people's empowerment but is actually totally imposed by central government on the orders of another central power, namely the Bank or the Fund.

Also, arguments about people's empowerment sit uncomfortably in documents which continue to belabour the need for external orientation. "If Africa's economies are to grow, they must earn foreign exchange to pay for essential imports...they must increase their share of world markets...higher export earnings must come from increased output."(LTPS p 13). So people's empowerment is directed not at greater self reliance and sustainable development, but at further entry to world markets where resistance to imports creates a hazardous trading environment. This seems to be the real motive for political conditionality.

The Western powers are increasingly and openly pressing for democracy in Africa. But the Bank goes beyond that, stressing the need for "empowerment" and "strengthening local organisations" rather than the usual promptings for political pluralism, human rights and democratic openings. Does this mean a real change of position by the Bank, or is it mere rhetoric ?

The answer seems to be that the Bank, like many other agencies, is linking criticism of African governments with proposals for other mechanisms for advancing development. There might be much to commend this view if it were part of a total strategy in which the role of government was given a place consistent with a genuine national development programme involving the people as a whole. But the LTPS does not support such a view, rather it is concerned with pressing private initatives against those of the state. It urges "a shift from central planning to a market-oriented approach, from regulation to competition".

Furthermore the proposals are all in the context of the firm disciplines of structural adjustment which are centrally and externally imposed, and have nothing to do with people's empowerment. Even this report states that SAPs "are important steps in the right direction" (p62). And there is a clear statement that this does not mean self-reliant and sustainable development on the basis of people placing their own needs first. "If Africa's economies are to grow, they must earn foreign exchange to pay for essential imports, etc. "(see quotation above). Individual initiatives are directed to free markets, not only internally but for international penetration.

Salim Salim, Secretary General of the OAU, has taken up the argument about political conditionality, saying that much of it is diversionary, though he does accept the case for greater empowerment and democracy.

The essential point, he argued, is that: "No matter how many political parties an African state may have, it will not change the price of coffee, cocoa, cotton, sisal or copper". (Speech at the House of Commons Conference in June 1990). He went on to say that greater African democracy would not reduce external dependency, nor lead to subsidising the rich of the North or the injustices of the poor of the South. In short, he suggested that it would be more appropriately linked to the democratisation of the international system.

This is the heart of the hypocrisy of the World Bank's position. Seeking to place the primary blame for Africa's condition on "poor governance" and lack of democracy, it nevertheless pursues policies which are so onerous on ordinary people that only repressive government can make them stick. At the same time the Bank supports international measures which are grossly discriminatory against the South and prevent any escape from underdevelopment.

THE CONTEXT FOR CHANGE

Instead of blaming governance, the IMF should take initiatives to create a NEW INTERNATIONAL ECONOMIC ORDER which would not allow net flows from South to North and which will open Northern markets to Southern exports at fair prices. At the same time, serious attention should be given by Africa to the question of empowerment and the social conditions required for change.

The evidence of the deterioration of Africa's condition is now well established. Popular protests are commonplace on the continent, sometimes verging on rebellion against authoritarian regimes. Inspiration for this opposition is often derived from the popular rebellions against authoritarian rule in Eastern Europe, where the people took to the streets to overthrow systems which had become stagnant and had failed to deliver on the promises of socialism. Likewise, the courageous resistance in South Africa has inspired the masses in Africa with the belief that repressive minority regimes must be substituted by democratic systems with empowered peoples.

One expression of this surge for democracy is the demand for multiparty systems which is finding expression throughout the continent. While it is evident that multipartyism cannot in itself be a guarantee of democracy, and indeed countries like Senegal confirm this point, it is clear that one party rule has been disastrous for Africa. In the early years of independence, leaders like Nyerere argued persuasively that it was possible to have clear choices between candidates and positions which would allow democracy to grow while yet avoiding the divisiveness of party politics. As the years passed, the one party system became increasingly ossified and power concentrated in the party leadership or even with the President himself. The state bureaucracy garnered as much power as it could, stifling initiative everywhere.

It is in this context that it must be conceded that the "liberal" call for multipartyism, even though often advanced by bourgeois forces in Africa, and endorsed by Western capital and agencies, represents a positive idea which can assist in breaking the stagnant mould of African politics. While we must agree with President Chissano that "If we have anti-democratic parties, then we will not yet have achieved the democracy we want" and "sovereignty resides in the people", the present momentum is nevertheless helpful. It creates the necessary political space for the articulation of new thinking about empowerment and development which is sorely needed.

It is also helpful that the Economic Commission For Africa (ECA) and the Organization of African Unity (OAU) are pressing for a new approach to development. Both are urging the democratisation of society and the empowerment of ordinary people. In doing so they are breaking down the reservations that have grown up about the role of African governments and official institutions over the past decade, as neocolonialism was seen to settle like a dead weight over the whole continent.

It is now possible for a wide range of progressive organisations to speak a similar language to these two bodies on the subject of development on the basis of a kind of consensus. The People's Charter adopted at the Arusha Conference of African NGOs, the Dar es Salaam Declaration of IFAA and the more recent Bulawayo Declaration of the Linking Conference are all good examples of new thinking about popular participation in development. Africa's NGO movement has to take up the campaign for empowerment and democracy, though on its own terms.

REQUIREMENTS FOR CHANGE

The classical view of development is that an economy must generate surpluses which can be invested productively. Often this meant restricting consumption to increase investment and the state was allocated this role, especially in centrally planned economies. More recently greater emphasis has been placed on the pattern and rate of accumulation. The state is supposed to have an accumulation strategy which is characterised by the kinds of social and economic investments it makes or encourages. It is vital to know how these are financed and who decides.

These matters have not been carefully defined in the typical neocolonial economy in Africa. Accumulation by the state and by the classes in and around the state has been misdirected and misallocated without serious reference to how the economy might develop. Instead, the state's preoccupation has been with resource extraction, social control and the personal empowerment of its managers, and this can only be done by authoritarian rule. Nzongola Ntalaja argues that many African rulers have virtually privatised the state itself in the sense that state resources, including state enterprises are used, not to promote the public good but to serve private interests. (Presidential Address ASA, October 1988).

The distortions brought about by these activities are serious. In the past decade in particular there has been massive capital flight, not only by foreign transnational corporations, but by the state and the elite. Additionally, vast resources have been wasted on useless prestige projects - modern hotels, party headquarters, ill conceived industries and enterprises which bear no relation to the real needs of the economy. Furthermore, elite consumption of luxuries has been a continuing drain on resources. In none of these instances has accumulation fed back into the economy productively or benefitted the people as a whole.

The central problem of these economies is that the masses do not participate in expanding the economy in accordance with their immediate needs nor is there an incentive system, political or economic, which would drive in that direction.

On the other hand the argument that democracy is necessary for development has yet to be proven rigorously. Too often it is a mere cliche used rhetorically. The problem is that it is patently obvious that some of the most rapid strides in growth have been achieved in societies with the worst records of economic exploitation. South Africa, for instance, made enormous strides on the basis of a forced and cheap labour system which laid the basis for industrialisation.

It is quite clear that the Bank does not object to cheap labour; on the contrary it is one of the pillars of structural adjustment.

Nor has the contemporary African one party system been favourable to a fair wage economy. Rather, labour has been co-opted and coerced in the spirit of capitalist accumulation, though the beneficiaries have not always been capitalist entrepreneurs but more often parasitic bureaucratic power groups at the top.

An undemocratic system can generate growth in the short term but it cannot produce development for the people as a whole since this requires peoples acquiesence and positive participation, though this is not an easy case to establish. But it is surely enough for us to justify empowerment and democracy on the grounds of equity and humanity.

EMPOWERMENT AND JUSTICE

The widespread concern about poor governance in Africa, the massive loss of legitimacy and popular support for most African states is of great concern. We do not need critics like the World Bank to sermonise on this for us. There has been so serious a loss of momentum for development, so much corrosion of infrastructure that even if these states were to muster a development policy with some credibility it is most unlikely that it would be implemented.

Yet it is clear that the state is an essential component of development. While previous dependence on the state was excessive, to the point where most other components were disregarded, there is no getting away from the need for state intervention, and not only in the provision of social infrastructure. Only the state can provide the support necessary to boost production in agriculture, the mainstay of the economy. Also, only a progressive state can give an impetus to the liberation of African women on the basis of a recognition of their real contribution to the economy.

Talk of the empowerment of ordinary people must take account of this reality. Therefore, while it is extremely valuable that so many writers on development and so many agencies of all kinds talk about people empowerment and emphasise grassroots components, to the point where it is suggested that grassroots projects might by themselves be the path to development, this is sometimes taken to extremes. Development is a complex process involving the whole society and all its material and human resources in a complex interplay. Indeed, to argue otherwise is a utopian illusion which can only lead into a cul de sac; similarily, with the notion that non-governmental organisations in Africa may be the main vehicle for development. Here again, it is to be welcomed that wholesale reliance on the state as the only actor in development has been overcome. But it is too optimistic to rely on NGOs which are isolated, fragmented and often at the mercy of state interference and denial of resources. That they might play a leading, even primary role in development, must be illusory. By all means let us press for the empowerment of the NGOs, even as a counterweight to the state, but this alone will not achieve the kind of transformation that Africa needs.

We are still left with the problem of transforming the state itself, and the way it functions, in order to achieve a humane society and one that is based on morality and integrity. Indeed it is the loss of moral values which is most suffocating in Africa today, just as it was this which brought the downfall of Eastern Europe's regimes.

COALITIONS FOR EMPOWERMENT

We conclude therefore that development requires a political approach. What is needed is the generation of political will leading to correct political choices.

We have to reject the structural adjustment approach of the LTPS report since it cannot generate the kind of political environment where real empowerment and popular participation in development will be possible.

Indeed opposition to structural adjustment could be the unifying factor for a whole range of political opinion which could form a coalition for an alternative path. The shape of such a coalition is apparent, including the OAU, ECA, various governments, and the whole spectrum of non-governmental and social movements. In the North there is also a substantial body of opinion, some of it well organised, in NGOs and the like, which is taking quite helpful positions in exposing and opposing the G7 power group as well as the Bank and Fund, the EEC and the rest.

Parallel with the above it is necessary to identify and mobilise social forces in Africa, across a wide spectrum including religious organisations, trade unions, women's groups, peasant associations, academics and so on.

It is urgent that the spontaneous protests of the last few years be given shape and content. This can only occur through the emergence of policy conscious organisations with programmes based on careful analysis. The relative absence of this kind of activity gives the impression that Africa is in the doldrums, unable to voice its aspirations. Public opinion needs avenues to make itself heard on the continent and internationally. In a sense this is perhaps the most significant dimension of the concept of "people's empowerment".

We need large coalitions within Africa and beyond to press for sound policies, for social transformation and development. Only then can we really transcend the politics of adjustment advocated by the World Bank.

THE LTPS & THE FRASER REPORT ON THE ROLE OF WOMEN

Emy Siganga

Firstly, I cannot see how the committees which produced the LTPS and the Fraser Report failed to find a single woman on the entire continent of Africa to serve on them and represent the interests of women. This was a terrible mistake. This is why we have such weak recommendations on the well-being of the silent majority. For this reason I condemn these reports. Women should be taken seriously and their opinions solicited before such bodies claim to know what women want and what they should do.

Secondly, the paragraphs on women in these reports emphasize the image of women as peasants. We know that, like anybody else, women have ambitions but these reports confine women to the agricultural sector. They talk about women's contribution to staple food production as if this is all that women will be doing in the 1990s.

Both reports acknowledge that over 60% of production is by women, and the LTPS admits that half of African farms are women-managed but not owned, for example the Congo where 70% of farms are managed by women. Then they go on to say that this is a limited contribution. What would the World Bank consider to be a full contribution? Given the primitive technology available to them and their reproductive role women make a large contribution to food production. By expecting a 100% contribution from women these reports are confining them to the non-monetary sector. Yet the issue, they say, is empowering women. For this to occur it goes without saying that women have to enter the monetary sector.

The Fraser Report identifies the legal structure, especially in respect of property rights, as being the main constraint to women's contribution. But it excuses African governments for the difficulties they face in instituting legal reforms. What is so difficult about this? It is high time we had legal reforms to cater for women's property rights. But by shifting the focus to an internal matter of states the Report remains silent on the issues of availability of resources and patterns of distribution to women. What of our sisters from nomadic communities? – we cannot talk about land tenure rights for them. How can they increase milk production? The Report is silent.

The major thrust of the two reports, in the few paragraphs in which they have highlighted the role of women, seems to be concerned with women as the major producers of staple foods and the need for them to remain as such, as this is what they can do. But, as I have said, this is false. Women have aspirations in other spheres and we shouldn't box them into the agricultural sector. Doing so creates a problem . If these reports are adopted, from now on it becomes more difficult for a woman to go elsewhere. She is told:

> *"You are supposed to be cultivating, women are not meant to go to university. You get your primary education and then you divert to where the World Bank is telling you to go."*

The Reports do not give us any strategies beyond that. This is totally unacceptable. They are confined to a few areas rather than being viewed holistically. The Reports don't touch upon matters of concern to women such as affordable technology, education and health care. Both reports seem to be preoccupied with agriculture. Women of Africa are also concerned with commerce, industry, trade unions and international issues.

Research and farmers training centres take very few women and even those they do take do not go into extension work. We need middle-level women extension officers, though we must avoid the danger of confining women to this sector. We should also be encouraging women to look ahead to using energy efficient electrical aplliances and not just talking about fuel saving stoves as the LTPS does.

The LTPS advocates further funding for education and yet Structural Adjustment Programmes have tied our hands by cutting down on funding for education. When parents have to choose between which child to send to school it is the girl who'll be told to get married because there are no fees, and goods will be sold to send the boy to school.

By confining women to subsistence farming the Reports perpetuate the old story of women's inability to participate in commodity production. But how can we empower women without their participation in commodity production?

In fact, women do contribute substantially to cash-crop production, they pick coffee and tea; cultivate tobacco and sugarcane, though the World Bank considers this "limited participation".

The United Nations Decade of Women and subsequent struggles have been about women's vision for getting out of the crisis and their centuries old marginalization, and yet the LTPS continues to marginalise women. It must be rejected.

A STRATEGIC AGENDA FOR THE 1990s

Abdoulaye Bathily

Something has emerged very clearly from these deliberations. The policies of the World Bank, the Uruguay Round and the Fraser Report are all aimed at the destruction of African social formations, though this is not acknowledged by their officials. We have here a clear cut case of a political economy of regression being set in motion by the trans-national corporations.

It is obvious that these policies will not bring happiness to the African people. They will not bring socialism, though of course we cannot expect the World Bank to bring socialism to Africa. But what is worse, the World Bank, the IMF and related multi-national institutions will not even bring capitalism to Africa. They will destroy the social, economic, political and cultural fabric of the African people.

From our deliberations it is clear that the economy of Africa is already suffering from these policies.

In my own country, Senegal, in the last four years one quarter of the labour force in industry has disapeared. Hundreds of factories have been closed as a result of the so called New Industrial Policy designed by the IMF and the World Bank. Food dependency has increased . The education system has been put in jeopardy. What we see in the field of education is a policy designed to transform the African people into unskilled labourers for international capitalism. This is the picture throughout Africa.

This reminds me of discussions we had over twenty years ago at Dakar University after the 1968 Movement in Dakar, when as students we were asking for reform of the education system. The government, under pressure, agreed to meet the Student movement and the Teachers Organization. A National Commission for Education Reform was set up in which students and other democratic forces advocated an education system to meet the needs of the African people. And the representative of big business, the French Chamber of Commerce in Dakar, had this to say:

> *"We agree with the students. We want an education system which matches the African reality. For instance, why should you Africans accept an education system which produces high ranking engineers, experts in the most sophisticated areas of research, when France can provide this for you. What you Africans need is good technicians. Industry in Senegal needs good laboratory technicians. This is what Africa should give to us and we will take care of the rest."*

When I read this report of the World Bank I recognised exactly the same colonial policy. Primary education has to be promoted but not higher education, no scientific research. How can we develop Africa without scientific and technical research at the highest level possible? We need engineers to tackle the problems of our soils in arid lands. We need medical doctors trained to look into the sort of diseases we have in Africa. But what do you find if you go to our Universities? That most of our doctors, though highly competent, are doing research on coronary thrombosis, a disease of the well to do people of Europe. What about malaria? What about the ordinary diseases that kill millions of Aficans year in and year out? This is a problem.

It is clear from the deliberations of the World Bank and its related institutions that they are pursueing a policy designed to consolidate and perpetuate the dependency of the African people. As a historian what I am saying is that what is happening in the 1990s is what happened to Africa a century ago. A new Berlin Conference, now in Washington, is taking place. In the 19th century Africa was being shared out among the European powers. In the 1990s it is as if an all-out re-colonization was taking place, not on the basis of traditional imperial values, but by common and protracted policies of the trans-national corporations.

The World Bank and its related institutions are not interested in the political development of Africa. They are not interested in democracy as such. Throughout Africa their policies are implemented in the most authoritarian way. Where is there room for parlimentary democracy or room for debate before implementing their policies? These are the marks of bourgeois democracy. Which parliament in Africa discusses IMF policies? Not one. We are ruled by foreign experts and their local proxies. This is not democracy.

When I say that the IMF and World Bank are not interested in democracy I mean they are not interested in governments which will be accountable to their people. We can see examples of this in several countries. Take the cases of Benin and the Ivory Coast, for example. The Prime Ministers, their governments, all of them are IMF boys. These are governments of technocrats, proxies of the IMF and World Bank, not governments that will be accountable to their people.

The fundamental question remains: What is there to be done? It is a classical question but we still have to pose it. A century ago when Africa was about to be plunged into the colonial night, the African people were submerged by the military might of the European conquerers. But at the same time they were in most cases betrayed by a number of their leaders who were competing for power for themselves. Their rivalries were used by the colonial conquerers to win acceptance for their administration. I think we have to draw some lessons from this era of our history.

In the 1990s, the new Berlin Conference – the new scramble for Africa, has subjected Africa to reports on its economic development. No other region in the world is subject to this kind of prescription. We have to adopt a common position. That is our historic task.

The question of UNITY is very much on the agenda. Unity on the basis of the alternative program for real recovery of Africa. Starting with what the Economic Commission for Africa (ECA) and the Organization of African Unity (OAU) have done we have to pull together all forces. Intellectuals have not only to investigate as we have been doing during this conference, but also to expose the policies and strategies of the IMF and World Bank. Trade Unions, and NGOs have to form a broad front, a coalition to fight against the IMF, the World Bank and related institutions and their local proxies. International pressure is needed but this pressure will find its allies within the continent itself. There is a need for the revival of Pan-Africanism, a new Pan-Africanism based on the lessons of the thirty years of independence, a new Pan-Africanism geared to the interests of the African people, a revolutionary Pan-Africanism which embodies the principles of real democracy, popular participation, a free press, freedom of speech and accountability of government to the people. These are some of the tasks facing the African people today.

THE WORLD BANK'S LTPS AND AFRICA'S TRANSFORMATION

Bade Onimode

"The experience of the first generation of Africans after independence raises some searching questions. Does Africa face special structural problems that have not been properly understood? Has the institutional dimension been neglected? Have the recent reform programmes been too narrow or too shallow? Could the process of formulating and implementing reforms be improved? Has the effect of external factors been correctly assessed? Are external assistance and debt relief appropriate and adequate? More fundamentally, is there a long-term vision that is both credible and energizing?"

(World Bank, LTPS, p.1)

1. PROLOGUE

These questions from the World Bank's major policy work, Sub-Saharan Africa: From Crisis to Sustainable Growth – A Long-term Perspective Study, demonstrate two significant facts. One is that the Bank itself has serious and nagging doubts about the positive impact and orientation of its policies in Africa over the past three decades. This is particulartly so because the SAP's of the 1980s were designed precisely to deal with these questions - or so we were told. That these questions should now arise reflects deep dissatisfaction with the Bank's own performance in African countries.

1.1 Consensus and Implementation

In the second place, these questions and much of the LTPS show that gradually, if belatedly, the Bank is coming round to contribute to the critical process of consensus building on some important solutions to Africa's problems. They reflect the emergence of significant areas of consensus between the Bank and its major critics in and outside Africa such as ECA, IFAA and others (LTPS, pp 1-2, 14-15). Areas of agreement bear recounting as evidence of progress away from the doctrinaire orthodoxy of on-going SAP's. They include: the need for adjustment with growth rather than the erstwhile insistence on stabilization before growth (though this is not equal to the development or structural transformation required by African countries); a human-centred development process and not mere economistic preoccupation with material things; the imperative of food security that still falls short of regional food self-sufficiency; democratic participation with equity; capacity building and regional self-reliance; and a long-term conception of development. But the proposed means of achieving these goals are still debatable and the areas of emerging consensus are yet to be translated into concrete policy actions and programmes.

Since the recovery and structural transformation of Africa is fundamentally the responsibility of Africans, and can only be assisted and supported from outside rather than being displaced or subordinated by foreigners, it is imperative that Africans subject the World Bank's LTPS and other external initatives to critical evaluation. This is to ensure that they do not displace or distort Africa's legitimate aspirations and proclaimed policy initiatives.

It is from this perspective that this paper finds the LTPS unwarranted, contradictory and therefore untenable as a policy option for Africa's development.

1.2 Untenable assumptions of LTPS

The World Bank's basic assumptions in LTPS are untenable in several respects. These assumptions include:

(a) Africa has no long-term perspective for its development hence the need for the World Bank's;

(b) Existing SAP's imposed by the IMF and World Bank should continue in spite of their catastrophic failure, and Africa should leave this area alone and start perspective programmes;

(c) The economic ideology of liberalism based on exclusive reliance on market forces and competitive pricing is best for Africa;

(d) The atomization of the state and informalization of the African economy is the best way forward;

(e) Peasant agriculture is the best option for the transformation of Africa's agriculture;

(f) People's development in the social services should be based on cost-recovery pricing in education, health, etc.

On the first false assumption that Africa has no long-term or perspective plan, the World Bank is pursuing a familiar course of always rejecting and opposing Africa's legitimate economic programmes. Thus when African countries, under the auspices of the OAU, adopted the Lagos Plan of Action (LPA) and the Final Act of Lagos (FAL) for Africa's economic development from 1980 to 2000 (a long-term perspective study), the World Bank rejected it and produced a counter-programme in the Berg Report titled Towards Accelerated Development in Sub-Saharan Africa which is outward-looking; when Africa prepared the African Priority Programme for Economic Recovery (APPER) for 1986-1990, for dealing with the crisis of the 1980s and the UN adopted it as the United Nation's Programme of Action for Africa's Economic Recovery and Development (UN-PAAERD), the World Bank and IMF produced an alternative Structural Adjustment Programme (SAP); and ten years after the production of the ECA's Long-term Perspective for Africa for 1983-2000, revised in the mid-1980s, the World Bank has now produced its own counter long-term programme in the LTPS. Why does the World Bank persistently reject and oppose excellent economic programmes by the OAU and ECA in preference to its own ? Who is the World Bank serving in Africa? The World Bank has to answer these questions unambiguously, especially since it maintains its empty rhetoric that "Africa's future can only be decided by Africans" (LTPS, p2).

Existing SAP's have failed disastrously, but instead of dealing with the mess, the LTPS invites African countries to give up their present in a grand diversion to the future - or as Keynes maintained, in the long-run we are all dead. Excessive reliance on economic liberalism in trade and other areas has been exerting heavy tolls on Africa since the 1980s, though Africa's structural rigidities have been repeatedly shown to be inconsistent with the competitive dreamland of Adam Smith as presented by the LTPS. It is not the business of the Bank to prescribe the Nordic model for Africa (LTPS, pp 186-7). The state is to be atomized and weakened by privatization and other measures in Africa, though it is being strengthened abroad. The informal sector, which should be subsidiary, is to become a dynamic force in Africa. This weak and disorganized sector is being proposed to lead Africa's industrialization - in the direction of de-industrialization without the medium and large scale core industries that transformed the advanced countries. Similarly, predominantly peasant production has not been known in history to transform the agriculture of any country as assumed in LTPS - hence the enclosure movement for large farms in Europe and co-operative farming in other parts of the world. The assumption that competitive cost recovery pricing of education, health and other social services will ensure human resources development is equally untenable. Orthodox SAP's have failed catastrophically in this regard with enormous human costs.

2. CAUSES OF THE AFRICAN CRISIS AND PROJECTIONS OF RECOVERY

On the basis of these false and unrealistic assumptions, the LTPS proceeds to a curious analysis of the causes of the socio-economic crisis and projects conservative growth targets.

2.1 Causes of the Crisis

The correct diagnosis of the causes of the crisis are critical to its effective and urgent resolution. Here the LTPS goes into deep economics and maintains: "the low return on investment is the main reason for Africa's recent decline" (LTPS, p3). It insists against all the evidence that the main causes of the crisis and decline in per capita income are internal. These are:

(a) falling export volumes, not falling terms of trade;

(b) excessive population growth; and

(c) low level and efficiency of investment (p3).

The net transfer of resources from Africa annually is over US$ 5 billion, including net transfers to the IMF and World Bank of over US$ 1 billion annually. The external debt service of over US$ 20 billion annually and the staggering debt service ratio of over 47 per cent in many countries is crushing. With the collapse of international commodity agreements in the 1980s there has been a calamitious fall in export prices that cost Africa's cocoa exporters an estimated US$ 150 million in 1990 alone. Foreign protectionism along with synthetic substitution have been the major causes of the decline in export volumes, together with the fact that when African countries increased their export volumes they realized less export revenue (e.g. Côte d'Ivoire during

1989-1990). Then, of course, the disarticulation of inherited colonial economic structures, the rising hostility of the international economic environment manifested in trade restrictions, increasing interest rates, deteriorating foreign lending conditions, etc. are all supposed to be insignificant. Even such internal factors as corruption and the siphoning off of huge funds abroad have mostly been perpetrated by unpopular regimes imposed on African countries by Western countries. Nobody denies the contribution of internal factors to the African crisis but its dominant causes are external, including failed World Bank and IMF policies like excessive generalized devaluation, import-substitution industrialization and the imperative of foreign capital in growth that led to the external debt crisis, etc.

2.2 Projected growth rates

In addition to the faulty policy prescriptions in the LTPS that derive from this partition analysis of the causes of the crisis, conservative projections for recovery have been suggested as follows:

PRODUCTIVITY

GDP	INDUSTRY	AGRICULTURE	OTHER SECTORS	LABOUR	LAND
4-5% at least	5% rising to 7-8%	4%	4-5%	1-2%	3%

Source: LTPS, p2

These projected annual growth rates are supposed to be based on historical trends and are seen to be 'highly ambitious'. Thus the LTPS states that the GDP has grown at an average annual rate of 3.4 per cent since 1961, but that there were variations across countries and over three periods: 1961/72, 'when incomes per capita grew', 1973/80, 'a period of stagnation' and 1981/87, 'a period of decline', (under SAP). By contrast, the ECA's long-term perspective for Africa has two scenarios: the projection of historical trends which it rejects because it might lead to a 'nightmare scenario' and the projection of normative trends that correspond to Africa's aspirations and some of the best achievements of the past. It is not surprising that by rejecting the ECA's normative trend projections, which yield higher growth rates, the World Bank concluded in its

1990 Report on World Poverty that Africa would be the only region in the world where per capita income would be falling right up to the twenty-first century. And why not, if Africa is to open up its economy fully to foreign pillage, depend mainly on peasant agriculture, rely on the informal sector for industrialization and start 'new generation SAP's'?

It must be emphasized that African countries greatly exceeded these conservative growth targets in the 1960s and 1970s, and, if recovery with transformation under massive reforms is to be meaningful, these growth targets must be exceeded in the 1990s. Nor are LTPS growth rates consistent, e.g. an agricultural growth rate of barely 4 per cent cannot support project agro-based industries that are to grow at 5 to 8 per cent.

3. NEW GENERATION SAP'S AND A GLOBAL COALITION FOR AFRICA

The LTPS has exceeded itself and showed its perverse intentions by calling for 'new generation SAPs' and a global coalition for Africa into the 1990s. These confound the real intentions of LTPS and the main interests that the World Bank seeks to serve and promote .

3.1 New Generation SAPs

The proposal that SAPs are still evolving (LTPS, p.xi), raises some urgent questions about old and new generations SAPs, i.e., SAP Mark I and SAP Mark II. Firstly, if SAPs are still evolving, why have the IMF and World Bank been so dogmatic about them, insisting on exclusive reliance on market forces and free pricing, trade liberalization, massive devaluation, high interest rates for the so-called positive real rate of interest, unwinding the state, doctrinaire privatization, etc., which have failed disastrously? Secondly, if African countries have in effect been used as guinea pigs for policy experiments in SAP Mark I, what is their compensation for the enormous losses suffered by them? What is the guarantee that in a few years, the new generation SAPs Mark II will also not be declared to be policy experiments? And for how long is Africa's development to wait while the World Bank amuses itself with these policy experiments at the expense of the lives of our people?

African countries have produced an African Alternative to IMF/World Bank SAPs in the form of An Alternative Framework to Structural Adjustment Programmes for Socio-economic Recovery and Transformation (AAF-SAP).

This AAF-SAP is intellectually superior to SAP and more relevant to the African context. So why is the World Bank not prepared to assist African countries to implement it rather than wasting resources on spurious alternatives?

Even the so-called new generation SAPs are problematic. Their moves towards consensus with African aspirations in AAF-SAP by allowing for more supply-side considerations, emphasizing human resource development, capacity building, democratization, etc. are yet to be implemented. Old SAPs are still very much in place without any sign of being replaced. While Africa is seeking long-term development or structural transformation, the LTPS is still preoccupied with mere growth - even in the long run. And Africa's long-term development objectives of regional food self-sufficiency, production integration, satisfaction of basic needs, etc. are yet to be accepted by the LTPS; its call for food security can be met by precarious food imports and food aid rather than domestic food production for food self-sufficiency as required by Africa.

3.2 A Global Coalition for Africa

The call for a Global Coalition for Africa (GCA) contradicts the LTPS rhetoric about Africans leading the process of regional development:

> "Can Africa's decline be reversed? The simple answer is yes... But it must happen from within Africa" (LTPS, p.194). Yet there is a call for 'a new international compact for Africa' - to build on the work of the UN-PAAERD initiative that ended in 1990. This Global Coalition for Africa is to be 'broader and more permanent. Its mandate would be to cover the full range of long-term development issues...' It would "be a forum of African leaders" and key foreign partners "to agree on general strategies that would then provide broad guidance for the design of individual country programmes" (LTPS, p 194).

This is effectively a demand for an alternative Economic Commission for Africa which we reject very firmly. The World Bank's preference for operating against the ECA and OAU's programmes like the LPA, APPER, etc. should not be used as a basis for suggesting that the ECA has not been effective and relevant to Africa - it has been more so than the World Bank. The 'full range of long-term development issues' and the 'generation of general strategies that would then provide broad guidance for the design of individual country programmes' is not the business of the World Bank or of any dubious Global Coalition for Africa. This is another grand design to disorient and derail Africa and we reject it. The proposed location of the Global Coalition for Africa in Europe with Robert McNamara, former President of the World Bank as its Chairman, reflects its basic inconsistency with Africa's aspirations and interests. The existing institutions for African development are adequate - if only the World Bank will stop undermining them and dismantling Planning Ministries and institutions in African countries. This must stop and the World Bank should be told firmly that it is exceeding its mandate and embarking on the recolonization of African countries which is unacceptable.

4. STRATEGIC AGENDA FOR THE 1990s

The last chapter of the LTPS elaborates a so-called strategic agenda for Africa in the 1990s. This is inconsistent with the World Bank's declarations that:

> *"Africa's future can only be decided by Africans. External agencies can play at most supportive role" and "... the reform programme is the government's" and "the reversal of Africa's decline must happen from within."*

If these statements are not empty rhetoric, why should Africa's strategic agenda for the 1990s not emanate from Africa? Since the OAU approved AAF-SAP and the LPA as Africa's strategic agenda for the 1990s and beyond, why does the World Bank prefer its own alternative agenda?

The LTPS strategic agenda is too narrow and too conservative for Africa's long-term development. African countries cannot make head way in the 1990s and beyond without the resolution of the external debt crisis. Yet the LTPS is silent on this central question.

The LTPS emphasises self-reliance and integration superficially. But its conception of integration is narrow, conservative and different from Africa's. The LTPS is silent on production integration, the key to the elimination of the structural root causes of Africa's protracted crisis. The market integration preached in the LTPS will only open up African markets for the products of the transnational corporations that have been exploiting, decapitalizing and impoverishing Africa for decades.

This so-called strategic agenda is also externally oriented. It focuses heavily on foreign donors and a foreign-dominanted Global Coalition for Africa, which will demobilize the internalization of Africa's development engine as called for in the LPA and other African blueprints.

The strategic agenda is suspiciously silent on food and agriculture, industrialization and the development of science and technology. Yet, these are among the priorities adopted by African countries for the region's agenda in the 1990s and beyond. Africa has been emphasizing human resource development and the promotion of core intermediate and capital-goods industries - even for successful agrarian transformation. But the strategic agenda sees only constraints and problems in the development of core industries (LTPS, p 187).

In these ways, it is clear that the LTPS so-called strategic agenda for the 1990s is a programme for the continued derailing of Africa's transformation - for the continued demobilization and marginalization of Africa. We reject it as too narrow, extremely conservative and suspect in other respects.

5. EPILOGUE

The World Bank's LTPS is a continuation of the Bank's chosen policy of opposition to, and rejection of, economic programmes and blue prints prepared and adopted by Africans themselves, valid and more relevant now than ever before. The LTPS raises the need to tell the World Bank to stop its counter-productive and wasteful policy of confrontation with the ECA, OAU and Africa's legitimate aspirations.

The false assumptions of the LTPS, its inconsistent policy directions and targets, its outward orientation and neglect of Africa's established development objectives make it largely irrelevant to the recovery and structural transformation of African countries.

Yet the indication in the LTPS of emerging areas of consensus between the World Bank and its critics is a positive aspect of the study. The opportunity should now be taken to implement these areas of agreement with respect to human resources development, the need for effective integration, capacity building in the development of science and technology, putting people first through democratic participation, etc. But these policy directions cannot be achieved by most of the means suggested in the LTPS.

SAPS AND THE GAMBIA

John Karimu

The advent of SAPs in the Gambia has had a profound and adverse effect not only on the lives of ordinary Gambians but on the operations of NGOs.

CUSO (Canadian Universities Support Organisation) started operations in the Gambia in 1973. At that time it was mainly a technical assistance agency bringing in Canadian volunteers to fulfill the manpower requirements of the different government ministries and other agencies. This was the basic agreement with the government up to 1983, when it was preparing to launch its SAP.

Until then we were bringing in 15-20 volunteers to serve in various ministries, mainly in education and health.

In 1984 the government put out a circular to all volunteer placement agencies making it clear that they were no longer interested in voluteers because there were an increasing number of local personnel to do the work they had been doing. This posed some initial difficulties but as a result CUSO in the Gambia decided to design an integrated village development program for the Upper River region, which had been neglected.

From then on all CUSO resources went into supporting projects within that program. In 1985 the SAP program was launched. The conditionalities that the Gambia had to implement almost immediately after the launch included the retrenchment of about 4,000 people from the civil service. This posed real difficulties for the government as it was short of people with the necessary skills to carry on its operations. This resulted in CUSO and other NGOs getting an increasing number of requests for volunteers to fill the vacancies not, as previously, on a cost sharing basis but fully funded by CUSO.

This poses a real problem for CUSO and means less money for our Upper River programs. It is difficult to get the government to understand that we have now changed our approach and prefer to work with community groups at the grassroots level addressing their basic needs. This issue is now under discussion between the government and TANGO, the coalition of NGOs in the Gambia. This problem is not confined to the Gambia but is also faced by CUSO in Ghana, Nigeria and Sierra Leone.

SAPs have also hit our work very directly, especially in the Upper River Division. Before SAP, groundnuts were the main cash crop. Cotton was produced, but on a very limited scale. Part of the package of SAP is to massively promote the production of cotton in this division, though it is precarious ecologically speaking. We are now reaching a situation in which cotton, produced for export to France, is taking over land previously used for food crops.

This has different consequences for different people: it means the men have much less time to assist the women in food crop production because of the time they are putting into cash crop production. It means the women, the main producers of food in the Gambia, are being pushed into the marginal lands. This is a serious problem but it is very difficult for a small NGO to fight the multinationals behind the production of cotton.

Before I came to this conference I attended a meeting with the Minister of Finance in which he gave us feedback on the new generation of SAPs. He opened his report by saying that he was pleased to tell us that our major donor, the World Bank, had had a change of heart. One thing that puzzles me in the Gambia is that despite all the negative effects of SAPs on the population, whenever you are invited to a meeting with the Ministries, you get the impression that the SAP program has been a success story. Official presentations use the usual macro-indicators. Frequently used examples are that since 1985 the Gambia has been able to generate enough external reserves to pay for 2 to 4 months worth of imports and has improved its debt servicing obligations. This is not set against the consequences such as those I have mentioned.

I have looked hard for a genuine assessment. At last I was lucky, and I laid hands on a document from a prominent minister in the Ministry of Planning and Finance. His assessment summarizes the actual situation and reinforces what has been discovered by the ECA and others. I would like to quote his concluding remarks from this document:

> *"improvements in the overall economy since 1985 have entailed adjustment costs for the economy and sacrifices for the population of the Gambia. At the end of the 1980s average living standards were still below the level reached in the 1970s. The*

> *burden of adjustment has been heaviest for those whose living standards were initially very low".*

This is the most accurate assessment of the situation. My impression is that policy makers do not fully understand the agendas of the World Bank and the IMF and they are being pushed into this kind of programme. Despite this assessment, in December 1990 the government launched a so-called "Program of Sustained Development" which, to all intents and purposes is a continuation of the first generation of SAP.

THE WORLD BANK'S NEW AGRICULTURAL POLICY FOR SUB-SAHARAN AFRICA

OR OLD WINE IN A NEW BOTTLE: WHAT HOPE FOR SUSTAINABLE GROWTH?

Ernest Maganya

"A central theme of the report is that although sound macro-economic policies and an efficient infrastructure are essential to provide an enabling environment for the productive use of resources, they alone are not sufficient to transform the structure of African economies...efforts are needed to build African capacities - to produce a better trained, more healthy population and to greatly strengthen the institutional framework within which development can take place".

(1989 World Bank Report on sub-Saharan Africa)

1. INTRODUCTION

The World Bank's (the Bank) 1989 Report on sub-Saharan Africa (SSA) titled "From Crisis to Sustainable Growth, a Long-term Perspective Study" has been hailed by analysts as a truly historic and controversial document. It raises for the first time the issue of governance and empowerment (Beckmen, 1990, Mistry, 1989).

The objective of this paper will be to assess the extent to which the 1989 Bank Report has made a radical departure from the orthodox Structural Adjustment Programmes so well articulated in the 1981 Bank Report on SSA. Before I can do so however, it is in order that I provide the context for this discussion.

In the early 1980s the Bank published a major report on SSA titled "Accelerated Development in sub-Saharan Africa, an Agenda for Action" (the Berg Report). This was followed by no less than five reports on the economic situation of Africa. As Mistry (1989) points out:

> "... it (the Bank) has produced a major report almost every eighteen months, Producing reports on Africa has become a completely independent cottage industry in the Bank".

With the possible exception of the 1989 Report, the rest were based on what has come to be known as the first generation of SAPs (FG SAPs). The FGSAPs were informed by macro-economic policies whose main objective was to restrict demand and switch it away from the production of non-tradeables to tradeables. Emphasis was therefore placed on the following key aspects:

1. correcting overvalued exchange rates through devaluation
2. replacing adminstratively determined interest rates by market determined interest rates (higher interest rate policy)
3. imposing credit ceilings on state owned commercial banks in order to restrict government expenditure particularly through marketing co-operatives and boards
4. the removal of inputs subsidies
5. the liberalization of produce marketing, and
6. the rationalization of state owned institutions through privatization and retrenchment of the working force.

These policies had a limited mandate - to restore the external and internal equilibria of African economies through increased exports and realigning government expenditure to income. Conspicuously missing were policies that addressed such key issues as human resources development, good governance and the responsibility of leaders to those they led, democracy and empowerment and, finally, the most urgent question of protecting the quickly deteriorating African environment.

This short term and highly technicist approach to solving the African socio-economic problems was challenged by UNICEF in its major publication on the need to have SAPs with a human face (Cornia, et al 1987). The argument was so well put that the Bank had to compromise. This led to a new acronym in the ever expanding vocabulary of the Bank - the Social Dimension of Adjustment

(SDA). In the case of Ghana, the first sub-Saharan African country to adopt and implement a SDA policy, a name that aptly summarizes the nature of SDA-type policies was chosen - Programme of Action to Mitigate the Social Costs of Adjustment (PAMSCAD).

As pointed out elsewhere (Othman, Maganya; 1990 and Beckman; 1990) the formulation of SDA-type policies only came as an after-thought and mainly as a result of tremendous pressures from the multi-lateral and bilateral community, mass resistance to some of the most distasteful SAP policies, and dissenting voices from small groups of articulate but highly influential academics in some SSA countries. The logic of orthodox SAPs, however, remained intact. Improvements in human capital continued to be regarded as the result of successful implementation of SAPs and not as part and parcel of the means, hence the mitigatory nature of SDA policy - a sort of time buying tactic! This point has been clearly articulated by Loxley thus:

> "It is a sad reflection on the Fund/Bank thinking that such considerations were not, and generally still are not, built directly into adjustment programmes. PAMSCAD was tacked onto the end of the body of the reforms package as a reluctant after-thought, under pressure from UNICEF and concerned bilateral donors". (Loxley, 1989).

This point has been brought up now because it is important in comprehending the nature of the human resources and political aspects raised in the 1989 Report, particularly as they relate to the agricultural sector.

Finally, our attempt to provide a contextual framework for our discussion would be incomplete without referring to the Economic Commission for Africa's seminal report "African Alternative Framework to Structural Adjustment Programmes for Socio-Economic Recovery and Transformation - AAF-SAP (ECA, 1989).

In our opinion, this short but incisive report raised the issues of human resources development, better governance, grassroots politics and the need to integrate all these in the process of formulating SAPs, in a way very few reports and other writings had done before.

The ECA report, while in principle accepting most of the macro-economic policies that are normally prescribed by orthodox SAPs, nevertheless, argued for a greater measure of flexibility in their implementation. Overvalued exchange rates should be devalued but not in a generalised manner and while budgetary reductions are indeed desirable, this should not be done at the expense of vital social services and essential consumer goods. The same case is argued for the credit squeeze which should not be indiscriminate and across the board, for the use of "selective nominal interest rates in a way that would ensure positive real interest rates for savings and finally for a less doctrinaire privatisation policy". (ECA, 1989: 36-43)

In view of the contextual issues raised above, can the Bank's 1989 Report be regarded as having ushered in a new era of a Second Generation of Structural Adjustment Programmes (SGSAPs)? The SGSAPs are supposed to integrate the short term imperative of stabilizing economies undergoing a deep economic crisis, with long term socio-economic transformation policies intended to bring about sustainable growth.

2. THE 1989 WORLD BANK REPORT AND THE AGRICULTURAL SECTOR

An interesting aspect of the 1989 Report, particularly as it relates to the agricultural sector, is its uncompromising stance on the policies that inform orthodox SAPs. In many ways, the 1989 Report has adopted a much more articulate and uncompromising position on market place policies than the 1981 Berg Report. We do not therefore quite agree with Mistry's (1989:18) most recent characterization of a timid Bank that hides its intention to undertake a major shift in the development paradigm (away from a particular form of collectivisation, a type of socialist mixed economy - sic!) behind the facade of adjustment policies.

Having enumerated a whole range of policies, including those on better governance, accountability, democracy and participation, the Bank ends the chapter on agriculture by pointing out that:

> "One constraint is Africa's lack of competitiveness. International markets for Africa's output exist. The challenge for Africa is to capture them by becoming more competitive. For that African governments will need to undertake the whole range of policies described above, but especially those concerned with exchange rates, marketing and technology." (World Bank, 1989:104)

It is not the objective of this short paper to review the major aspects of the macro-economic policies that inform orthodox SAPs. This has been done elsewhere (Maganya, 1988 & 1990). Suffice it to point out here that such key aspects as devaluation and high interest rates have had little or no positive impact on agricultural production in the more than thirty SSA countries now implementing SAPs. Even in those countries that are being depicted as success stories, like Ghana, the supply response to the price incentive seems to be of a short run nature and to be limited, in most cases, to one export crop (cocoa for Ghana, and cotton for Tanzania) (refer to Loxley; 1989 and Maganya; 1990).

It looks increasingly uncertain that the price incentive alone is a necessary and sufficient condition to enable the African peasant to cross the technological threshold that is so essential to ensure sustainable high levels of agricultural production. The message that one gets throughout the Report, however, revolves around two policy issues: 1. price incentives through an active exchange rate policy, and 2. privatization of every aspect of African agriculture from crop purchase to the adoption and popularization of appropriate technologies. The motto seems to be, "Seek ya first the economic freedom of the market place and everything else will be added unto you".

2.1 Privatizing the Agriculture Sector

The privatization of the African agricultural sector has been accorded such a prominent place in the report that we deem it fit to discuss it separately. To show how the Bank takes the issue of privatising the agricultural sector seriously, we have taken the liberty of identifying how many times and in connection with which agricultural practice the word "privatization" appears in the seventeen page chapter on agriculture.

Summarized below, is the occurence of this word and related agricultural practices:

i) The expansion of agribusiness in Africa through core-farm-smallholder relations (pg 93).

ii) Extending credit facilities to African farmers through financial intermediaries (i.e. through traders who sell farm inputs and equipment on credit (pg 94).

iii) The use of private voluntary organizations to introduce simple mechanical devices (pg 97).

iv) Provision of veterinary services by the private sector (pg 98).

v) The use of the private sector to import, produce and distribute chemical inputs (pg 96).

vi) Increasing fisheries capabilities through policies and financing that encourage the private sector involvement (pg 99).

It would be beyond the scope of this paper to discuss all the aspects of private practice in agricultural development of African economies suggested by the Bank's report. We would, nevertheless, like to emphasize one point and this concerns the pathological dislike of the role of the state in economic transformation shown in this chapter and, indeed, in the whole Report. It looks highly suspicious that the crusade against the state is not based on any concrete historical justification (either in Africa or elsewhere). While we would agree that in the specific experience of Africa the state has performed rather miserably in the economic sphere, the cure to the African catastrophic economic crisis cannot be through the unreserved embrace of the private sector.

Thus while we agree with the Bank that "Africa needs not just less government but better government... ", we take great exception to the Bank's assertion that the government should concentrate "... its efforts less on direct interventions and more on enabling others to be productive" (Bank, 1989). As in all other aspects of policy making in Africa, this cannot be an across the board affair . In certain areas, including the protection of the smallholder farmer against the not always productive and beneficial intervention of the commercial traders and big farmers, the state cannot afford to adopt a neutral stand.

This discussion brings us to the last part of this paper which deals with the much more controversial issues of participation, empowerment and democracy. These issues have a great bearing on the imperative of not only having a small and better government in the technicist sense but also providing what the Bank calls the "countervailing power" (pg 60).

3. GOVERNANCE, EMPOWERMENT AND HUMAN RESOURCES DEVELOPMENT - the art of grafting: concluding remarks.

One thing stands out clearly in the 1989 Bank's Report - the art of grafting. We have noted earlier how the Bank and the Fund, under extreme pressure from UNICEF, were forced to graft human resources development issues onto orthodox SAPs. Now it would seem, as a result of the clearly thought out arguments expressed in the ECA's AAF-SAP on empowerment, democracy and the need to indigenize the development process, the Bank has once more been forced to tack these concerns onto the end of the body of the reform package, to use Loxley's expression already quoted above. To us, this seems to be a very badly carried out transplantation exercise and there is every likelihood that the "body of the reform package" will reject these foreign bodies unless the package itself is radically tranformed.

One aspect is conspicuous by its absence from the whole discussion on empowerment, participation and accountability: grassroot resistance to certain aspects of orthodox SAPs, particularly those aspects that have greatly contributed to the erosion of the welfare of the majority of the African people. This silence is, of course, deliberate. It is intended to make people believe that the increased repression that normally accompanies these policies is mainly caused by the undemocratic practices of African governments.

That a reform of African government by making it smaller and better by, among other factors, the creation of a countervailing power (pg60) will make it more democratic and participatory, orthodox SAPs notwithstanding, is questionable. As Beckmman (1990) points in his very incisive paper on the politics of African adjustment, it is highly unlikely that the Bank would advise African governments to encourage organized grassroot politics. On the contrary, what lies behind the Bank's "politics" of adjustment is the creation of a powerful middle class (in the case of the rural areas, large scale farmers) with clearly defined economic and political interests and rights. It is expected that in the process of defending these rights, this middle-class would bring pressure to bear on African states and make them accountable to itself. This is the countervailing power, the so-called intermediaries (farmers, financiers, inputs-purchasers and distributers, NGOs, etc.) that feature so prominently in the Bank's Report. The Bank's disregard for grassroot politics can be clearly discerned in the following words;

> "Intermediaries have an important role to play; they can create links both upward and downward in society and voice local concerns more effectively than grassroots institutions. In doing this, they can bring a broader spectrum of ideas and values to bear on policy making. They can also exert pressure on public officals for better performance and greater accountability. (World Bank, 1989:61).

Here the logic of the Bank is flawed. Is it not true that the so called intermediaries can only be effective in creating "... links both upward and downward ..." if there are organized grassroot institutions? And what would be the motive of the Bank in claiming, against all available evidence, that intermediaries (i.e. local leadership, pg 61) are not exploitative?

By adopting this uncompromising position against the Bank's preoccupation with the new-found level for popular politics (remember the poverty-oriented policies of the 1970s?), we are not unaware of well-intentioned individuals and organized intermediaries (NGOs, Church Organizations, etc). These do exist and they normally perform wonderfully in empowering the poor. All we are saying is that they cannot by themselves be depended upon to bring about fundamental and sustainable political and economic transformation in the lives of the majority of the people of Africa. Here we have in mind the smallholder farmers. This is even more difficult so long as the Bank is content with the simple transfer of the old wine (orthodox SAPs) into the new bottle of empowerment, participation and accountability.

SELECTED BIBLIOGRAPHY

World Bank *Accelerated Development in sub-Saharan Africa, An Agenda for Action*, Washington DC, 1981.

Sub-Saharan Africa from Crisis to Sustainable Growth: A long-term Perspective Study, Washington DC, 1989.

Mistry, P. *The Present Role of the World Bank in Africa*, Institute for African Alternatives, London, 1989.

Loxley, J. *Structural Adjustment in Africa: Reflections on Ghana and Zambia*, Review of African Political Economy No. 47.

Cornia, G A; Jolly, N E; and Stewart, F (eds) *Adjustment with a Human Face: Ten Country Case Studies.* Vol I Clarendon Press, 1987.

Othman, H and Maganya, N E; "The Debt Problem in the context of the Third World, The case of Tanzania",
in Othman, H. and Maganya, N E; *Tanzania Debt crisis and the World Economy*, IDS, Dar es Salaam, forthcoming.

Maganya, N E; *Structural Adjustment Programmes and the Agricultural Sector: The case of Tanzania, Taamuli*, Vol 14, forthcoming.

Structural Adjustment Programmes and Smallholder Farmers in Tanzania: The Case of Mwanza Cotton Growers: Final Report presented to Organization for Social Science Research in Eastern Africa 2nd Competitive Research Award Project, 1990.

"Large and Small Scale Farmers: A paradigmatic inquiry into the Agricultural policies of Zimbabwe, Malawi and Tanzania," in,
Himmeletrant et al: *Controversies, Dilemmas and Openings in the Study of African Development: In Search of New Paradigms*, Sage Publications, forthcoming.

Beckman, B *Empowerment or Repression? The World Bank and the Politics of African Adjustment.*
Paper to a Symposium on The Social and Political Context of Structural Adjustment in Sub-Saharan Africa organized jointly by UNRISD, SIAS and CMI in Bergen, Norway, 17-19 October 1990.

FORGOTTEN ISSUES OF LTPS

Sam Oiro

My paper is entitled, "The Forgotten Issues of LTPS" because certain issues have either not been addressed adequately or have just been ignored. There is a growing acceptance everywhere that the issues confronting Africa's development are inter-linked. It is known that food security, education, health, the environment, technology and trade cannot be separated. The World Bank realizes this because there has been a lot of pressure on it to show genuine concern. The staff of the World Bank have started to pay lipservice to this concern. At the same time they say in the foreword of the LTPS (page 8):

> "this study by the staff of the World Bank and the judgments in it do not necessarily reflect the views of the board of directors or the governments that they represent".

That quote alone makes one wonder who makes policies in the World Bank and whether African development is outside the Board's policies.

Just after the launching of the LTPS, when opening the World Bank-IMF annual general meeting, President Conable showed great arrogance about the World Bank's past experiences in Africa's development:

> "we know a great deal about who the poor are, where the poor are and how they live. We understand what keeps them poor and what must be done to improve the quality of their lives."

That statement forms the basis of this LTPS and I wonder how many people here agree with Mr. Conable. From what we have seen, the Bank's belief is that economic growth is the cornerstone of development and poverty reduction and Structural Adjustment is the precondition for restoring growth in many countries. This theme runs through the LTPS. With this strategy the World Bank hopes to lift hundreds of millions of people out of poverty by the year 2000.

AGRICULTURE

Food Security has been defined elswhere as, "access of people to adequate, secure and healthy supplies of staple foods, produced on a sustainable basis at prices which all can afford".

The LTPS gives six strategies for doing this:

1. The private sector and the market have to be given the biggest role and administrative controls reduced. The market must be free, without any regulation at all.
2. Attention must be given to agricultural research and training, although these are not defined and no actual strategies are given. While they also emphasize the international aspects of research, no account is taken of talks that are already going on, even those under GATT, or of technology patenting and so on, that will emanate from such research.
3. The development of infrastructure and the maintenance of rural infrastructure needs to be given greater attention, with the participation of the beneficiaries. This presupposses that the masses of Africa have not been participating and that they have to do much more in the development of infrastructure. We all know what it costs to put infrastructure in place and we know the income levels of the poor .
4. Environmental protection issues like soil erosion, deforestation, watershed management and so forth must be addressed. But there is no mention of such issues as the effects of greater use of fertilizers and pesticides.
5. Programmes to assist women as farmers and traders should get government assistance.
6. Systems of land tenure should be reviewed.

In reaching the conclusion that the above strategies can pull Africa out of poverty, the LTPS has not given enough recognition to some important related issues:

1. The problem of hunger , food security and sustainabliity in Africa. The greatest cause of hunger is poverty and underdevelopment and therefore food security can only be guaranteed to the extent that the challenge of poverty, including international inequalities, is overcome. Food security may be guaranteed through food imports. You don't have to produce food yourself to have food security. But this strategy sadly misses the point that the present crisis in Africa is a highly complex affair, comprising not only food imports and

hunger, but large and growing external debts, severe shortages of foreign exchange, major deficits on state's budgets and the virtual collapse of economies.

The food problem is first and foremost a matter of declining incomes and increasing insecurity of food supply to the poorest people on the continent. Attempts to improve the situation by increasing overall production through the strategies suggested by the World Bank, without reference to distribution and international trade policy, far from improving matters are likely to make them worse. This applies not only to real incomes and food security but to longer term development goals.

Many of the projects currently being pushed through Project Aid pose great dangers to the African environment and to the long-term overall growth of production. Their effect in generating inequality is also likely to be marked.

2. The negative effects of the private sector and privatization on agricultural production, marketing and prices is not considered. While the World Bank report recognises that most food is at present produced by peasant farmers, it is adding to privatization in agriculture and sees private investment as playing a big role. However, it does not seem to have considered that agribusiness prefers crops which require the intensive use of pesticides or that they develop environmentally vulnerable mono-cultures. The profit drive and the emerging power of biotechnology make it possible that existing problems might be exacerbated by introducing crop substitution and actually undermining the export capacity of Africa. While the most efficient producers gain from internal trade liberalization, the poor will starve for want of purchasing power. The role of government in ensuring a fair system is still necessary, but, as you all know, this role is sidelined in the LTPS.

3. Agricultural trade policies, internationally and nationally, are also not considered because, even nationally, governments are not suppossed to stabilize prices. Access to markets and regional trade is not considered at all. Nor is the fact that the Uruguay Round of GATT negotiations will be capable of reversing any decisions reached elsewhere, even on the LTPS itself.

4. The fundamental role of research in agricultural development has been recognized by many. The importance of creating an adequate scientific and technological base in Africa is understood and desirable. However, the way in which it will be done is the biggest challenge. On page 99 the World Bank Report says:

"more has been spent on agricultural research in sub-Saharan Africa per farmer than anywhere else in the developing world."

The report quotes the figure of $360 billion against $190 million spent in Southeast Asia , where there are more farmers . If that is true they should look at what this sum was spent on. We know of several agricultural stations involved in research, in Kenya for instance. Some of them are in the middle of nowhere, so the infrastructure must have consumed most of that money. This infrastucture was in fact for the benefit of the experts who were recommended by the donors to man those stations. I am not saying all the money has been spent in this way, but most of it went to that kind of expenditure.

Secondly, if agricultural research is to be meaningful and progressive, issues of bio-technology and patenting, currently being discussed in GATT under TRIPS (Intellectual Property Rights) must be considered. There are suggestions that even seeds will be patented. Fortunately, I am told that indigenous seeds cannot be patented but anything that comes from that seed, like a hybrid, could be patented, which means that African countries would have to pay royalties on hybrid seeds.

I should therefore like to propose that the World Bank give much greater attention to the following points:

1. Recognition of measures such as price supports, export controls, tariffs, import prohibitions as legitimate and necessary instruments for Africa in its efforts to enhance domestic agricultural output and national or regional food security. These measures are not new. Europe still uses them against food imports from Africa and I don't see why they should not be relevant to agricultural production in Africa.

2. Essential government intervention for development purposes, such as the provision of reasonably priced inputs and credits, research and extension services and the assurance of renumerative and stable prices cannot be compared with the restrictive trade measures of industrialized countries. In fact, governments need to be empowered, through technical training, exposure and the provision of funds, to make these interventions.

3. The elimination of all measures by the major food exporters including European countries and the U.S. that lead to the export of agricultural products onto world markets at prices below production costs, as this represents a threat to Africa's food security. Since this would impose costs on the net food importing countries, I suggest some form of compensation for the higher world prices until domestic outputs increase. I think this is important because I believe that one of the problems of food production has been the low prices of

imported food. This might include price incentives for local farmers and financial aid to develop the agricultural sector's production, infrastructure, marketing and so on. Where possible food aid should be provided through triangular operations with the net food surplus coming from other African or developing countries.

4. Continuously falling prices of primary products have put a big strain on the development efforts of many African countries. The World Bank should in fact support other ongoing pressure groups to raise and stabilize world prices through commodity agreements that at the moment are falling down one by one. They should also strengthen current demands by African countries for more market access. Only then can we start finding ways to ensure that increased export earnings will directly improve the employment and income levels of the poor. At the moment we are talking from a theoretical basis because there is no income.

5. The World Bank should encourage and support meaningful African efforts towards the creation and extension of preferential trade arrangements such as the LOME trade agreements, and most importantly, sub-regional and regional economic integration within Africa. It is through this that Africa can trade among itself and realize its potential.

6. The World Bank should join hands with other pressure groups inside and outside Africa to make GATT and the people who control it understand that what Africa needs is FAIR trade and not necessarily free trade. Competition in trade under the current system has led to market acquisition involving winners and losers rather than mutual and reciprocal enrichment.

African countries and others must not be forced to fit into an overall scheme drawn up as though all contracting parties were equal partners. I think that if the World Bank, instead of just coming up with their program for Africa, joined in pressurizing forces elsewhere the effect would be more helpful .

It is also widely argued that the basis for the food crisis in Africa is the decline in per capita food production, the root cause of which is the rapidly increasing population while agricultural technology is stagnating. It is true that Africa's population is increasing, but there is little evidence that the problem lies in the overall disparity between population growth and food production. There is, however, a huge disparity between the delivery of food to official marketing agencies and urban food demand. If the problem was aggregate production then it would make sense, if the World Bank is correct , to seek a solution by the most rapid possible means including privatization, as the LTPS suggests. This would mean concentrating efforts on the people who can produce faster, that is, the richest agro-businessmen.

On the other hand, if the problem is that many areas and groups of people are steadily getting worse off, which is in fact the case, and producing less food per capita, with less security because of soil erosion or desertification, increasingly vulnerable to climatic variations, lacking incentives because of low prices, then increasing agregate production is not the answer. As the capacity to produce of the poor peasantry and the people in the marginal areas declines and becomes more insecure so does their income and capacity to buy food. Increasing aggregate food production may lower prices but it will not provide the incomes for those who cannot afford it. This can even worsen the situation of those who depend on selling food for cash.

Yet, this is what the LTPS seems to suggest.

One particularly dangerous formulation of development policy coming from the World Bank LTPS is the proposal of a strict division between economic and social aid projects. The former are to be effective by being concentrated on the best farmers, areas and crops. The latter, which are supposed to take care of regional and social disparities, enhanced by the former, concentrate on health,education, water supply and sometimes erosion control and agro-forestry.

There is nothing wrong with the latter type of project in principle but the impact of social aid projects is reduced or nullified where basic incomes and food supply are deteriorating; and social projects have a tendency to cluster in the better areas, as do projects for infra-structure, marketing, cooperative development and most of the other things that are suggested in the LTPS.

In short, building on the best, in the World Bank's words, and privatization for rapid agricultural growth is likely to undermine the poorest and make the real food problems worse.

Finally, I would like to pose a question. The LTPS was written and launched when the Uruguay Round was in progress. The World Bank must have known the implications of the negotiations – that they would subordinate everything to free trade and give multi-nationals access to every aspect of international trade – yet they chose to ignore them. Is this a matter of accident or intention?

BETWEEN LEGITIMACY AND DOMINANCE: THE AAF-SAP VERSUS THE IMF SYSTEM

Mohammed Nureldin Hussain

A. INTRODUCTION

Reading the policies prescribed by the "African Alternative Framework to Structural Adjustment Programmes" (AAF-SAP), we could not resist the temptation to figure out those policies that are in conflict with IMF basic rules (i.e. the rules that are explicitly stated in the IMF Articles of Agreement). Having found out that one or two can be classified as being in full violation of IMF rules, we went a step further to find those in conflict with IMF economic philosophy; those that require additional foreign exchange; and those that necessitate radical internal political decisions.

Building on the above classification the paper attempts to explore the real challenges facing the adoption and implementation of AAF-SAP by African countries. The paper is organized as follows: Section B gives an overview of the IMF rules, Section C attempts to refute the illegitimacy of AAF-SAP. Section D explores the interrelations between the dominance of the contemporary IMF system and the need of AAF-SAP for foreign exchange and for radical political decisions. The concluding remarks are provided by Section E.

B. CONTRASTING THE TWO MODELS

B.1 The IMF Model

It has become a common practice among academics and policy makers to describe and analyze the IMF model by referring to the policies prescribed by the IMF. Accordingly, the recipe of currency devaluation supported by demand management policies came to be known as the standard IMF model. In the literature on the subject, the IMF diagnosis receives very little attention. In this paper, an alternative approach is adopted. The IMF model is described and examined with reference to IMF diagnosis of balance of payments disequilibria. By this approach we hope to reveal more of the economic wisdom backing the IMF prescription and show how this wisdom contrasts with that of AAF-SAP.

The predominant facet of any IMF stabilization programme is the fight against inflation. It is because of this emphasis on inflation that the early IMF policy packages were termed "stabilization programmes" (Payer 1974). In the IMF policy diagnosis, domestic inflation is the result of increases in money balances in excess of increases in the volume of goods and services in the economy. Excessive money balances are identified with government deficit financing and the expansion of bank credit. According to the Fund, domestic inflation adversely affects the balance of payments through two main routes:

(a) the effect of inflation on capital flows;

(b) the effect of inflation on relative prices (or what the IMF calls inflation-induced distortions of the market forces and the pattern of trade).

Domestic inflation is said to have two major effects; first it discourages the inflow of capital particularly in the form of direct foreign investment, since it causes considerable uncertainty regarding the future level of money costs and money receipts on foreign investments. Additionally, inflation in the home country is said to lead to the adoption of foreign exchange restrictions which by themselves frighten capital away and encourage capital flight through repatriation. (Dorrance 1965).

In the IMF standard kit of analytical tools, distortions of the market forces and the pattern of trade arise because rapid domestic inflation causes the prices of goods in the leading sectors of the economy to lag behind the general price level. Although it is difficult to make any generalization about the manner in which inflation distorts relative prices and how this affects the balance of payments, the Fund often identifies three sets of prices as the worst affected. These are:

(a) what the IMF calls "political" prices which include prices of public utilities, public transportationrates, prices charged by public enterprises, and prices of necessary goods controlled by the government to protect lower income groups;

(b) real interest rates; and

(c) the exchange rate which determines the relative prices between foreign and domestic goods.

Any government policy which aims at protecting poor consumers against rising costs and prices is regarded by the Fund as artificial suppression of inflation which distorts market forces leading to inefficient allocation of resources. These measures are held responsible for the underdevelopment of important components of the economic infrastructure as well as the underdevelopment of the agricultural sector whose prices are said to often fall victim to such measures. Furthermore, subsidization and underpricing of public utilities are said to undermine the profitability of public enterprises and to increase the government deficit, thereby resulting in a further rise in inflation.

The second set of prices which inflation is said to influence are real interest rates. As inflation proceeds, real interest rates are said to become inadequate or even negative. This is said to discourage domestic savings in financial forms and hence impede the development of financial intermediaries and capital markets. In addition unrealistic rates of interest are said to have adverse effects on the level of savings as a whole. The effects of inflation on "political" prices and real interest rates are asserted to affect the balance of payments indirectly through excessive government deficits and the sluggish growth of output (Polak 1968).

Distortion of the pattern of trade, in the IMF literature, refers to the effect of domestic inflation on the exchange rate. Under fixed exchange rates, domestic inflation is said to render the local currency overvalued. The Fund's views on the effect of an overvalued currency are best represented by the following statement made by an Executive Director of both the IMF and the World Bank:

"... The maintenance of an unrealistic exchange rate - it is hardly necessary to stress that in this context I mean an overvalued one - distorts the pattern of foreign trade, in that it stimulates imports by making them unduly cheap, and hampers exports by making them unduly expensive abroad. This by itself retards economic growth as it puts production for exports in an unfavorable international position... in addition it adversely affects the balance of payments and this calls for contractionary internal measures unless trade and payments restrictions are introduced. In either event the condition for maximizing the rate of economic growth is far from being attained". (Lieftinck 1964)

It can, thus, be argued that in the IMF diagnosis, external deficits are essentially caused by rapid domestic inflation. The standard IMF prescription emerges as a logical outcome of such diagnosis. Devaluation is prescribed to correct the overvalued exchange rate (and hence encourage exports and discourage imports) and to restore confidence in the national currency (and hence encourage capital inflow and discourage capital flight). The anti-inflationary policies are prescribed to stop inflation from undermining the new exchange rate. And the inflationary-deflationary policies (including the removal of subsidies and price decontrols) are prescribed to correct price distortions by increasing the real prices of the leading sectors of the economy, paving the way for the promotion of growth.

This IMF diagnosis and prescription has remained unchanged despite the IMF's move from "Stabilization" to" Structural Adjustment" in the post-oil crisis era. The shift to Structural Adjustment had two basic features. First, the period of Fund programmes was lengthened by the introduction of the Extended Arrangement, the Structural Adjustment Facility and the Enhanced Structural Adjustment Facility which have time periods of 3 years or more. Second, debt management in the form of ceilings relating to maturity, and terms on the acquisition of new external debt became an important element of IMF performance criteria (Hussain 1983).

Apart from these cosmetic changes there were no alterations in the IMF policy-mix. The structural change of African countries is to be realized by the same standard model of devaluation and anti-inflationary measures – with the difference that devaluation is now viewed not merely as an instrument of development policy, which allows a proper choice of production techniques and promotes economic growth through the expansion of the export sector (Hussain 1983).

B. 2 The AAF-SAP Model

Unlike the IMF model, AAF-SAP does not view external deficits of African countries as caused by the arithmetic of inflation. External deficits are seen by AAF-SAP as the final product of the state of underdevelopment of the economies and societies of African countries. While the IMF model sees external deficits as the product of domestic inflation, AAF-SAP treats external deficits together with inflation as two of the many symptoms of underdevelopment. Thus, for AAF-SAP external adjustment in the context of African countries, can only be achieved through development.

Using the world "deficit" to mean the deficiency of what is available compared with what is required, African countries suffer from many persistent deficits apart from the balance of payments; in education and training services, in health services, in food, in production-servicing facilities and in productive capacity, to name a few. An arithmetic correction of the external deficit alone can only be achieved at the expense of exacerbating these development-related deficits. Alternatively, AAF-SAP aims at adjusting external deficits through an integrated development-related adjustment. Viewed as such, AAF-SAP is based on development and adjustment .

It attempts to eliminate the dichotomy between Structual Adjustment and long-term development. Adjustment is seen as part of a continuous process of development rather than a discontinuous exercise on its own. To achieve sustained development it is necessary to ensure the transformation of the society and economy through education, training, health and well-being and vitality of the people so that they can participate fully. AAF-SAP postulates that the path of adjustment with transformation should aim at simultaneously strenthening the process of income generation, distribution, and expenditure.

With respect to income generation, AAF-SAP calls for "a more human-centered development process in which production forces are given a predominant role, and resources are used so as to bring about the transformation of the African economy from a primarily exchange economy to a production economy." (p 29).

To this end, the major policy directions are: improving human resource capacity, enhanced production and efficient resource use, greater and more efficient domestic resource mobilization, strengthening the scientific and technological base and vertical and horizontal diversification.

As for income distribution, AAF-SAP focuses on ensuring a greater and more effective involvement of socio-economic institutional groups in the process of adjustment with transformation. The main policy directions in this area are: establishing a pragmatic balance between the public and private sectors; improving the pattern of income distribution, shifting resources towards productive activities, and creating an enabling social, economic and political environment for sustainable development.

Regarding the expenditure of national income, AAF-SAP focuses on the satisfaction of basic needs, improved accessibility to essential goods and services, and increased domestic production of essential factor inputs. The major policy directions in this field are the attainment of food self-sufficiency, lessening import consumption and imported inputs dependence and managing debt and debt services.

To achieve the above policy directions, which aim at adjustment with transformation, AAF-SAP prescribes a set of policy instruments and measures.

C. ON THE LEGITIMACY OF IMF RULES

In the sphere of the satisfaction of critical needs AAF-SAP prescribes "utilizing the existence of de facto multiple exchange rate systems in a rationalized manner and/or creating and streamlining such a system for purposes of resource transfers, resource mobilization and reversal of capital flight and ensuring availability of essential imports".

This measure is in clear violation of IMF Articles of Agreement. Article VIII states that: "No member may without the approval of the Fund, impose restrictions on making payments or transfers for current international transations or engage in discriminatory currency arrangements or multiple currency practices".

As it is well known, this Article – which forms one of the important principles of the Bretton Woods System – was based on the USA's hostility to the trade and exchange restrictions of the 1930s. The USA wanted the international post-war system to be open to its trade and investments.

But what is desirable for the economy of the USA in the past or present, is not necessarily desirable for African countries. In the context of AAF-SAP, discriminatory currency practices can be efficiently used to foster inter-African trade. Also, multiple exchange rates can be used to provide incentives for selective exports and workers remittances , and to encourage the import of selective capital goods, avoiding at the same time the undesirable consequences of blunt devaluations .

Although the principle of free trade and exchange is an important constituent of the Bretton Woods philosophy, the solid foundations of the system is provided by two other closely related rules. In order to fulfill the purposes enumerated in its first Article of Agreement, the IMF was supposed to guarantee the gold base of the system as a whole and the stable parities of the currencies of member countries. But both rules were abandoned because they ran into conflict with the functioning and the interests of Western economies.

The Bretton Woods' fixed exchange rate system and its gold base came under attack during the late 1960's and early 1970's because of the growing monetary interdependence among the major Western economic powers. This was mainly due to the growing international structure of production characterized by the expansion of multinational corporations. Other sources of monetary interdependence were the internationalization of commercial banks and the creation of the market for Eurocurrencies, which is a form of uncontrolled capital market with highly mobile short-term funds.

These forms of interdependence had profound effects on the functioning of the international as well as domestic monetary systems. The Western countries, committed by the Articles of Agreement to maintain fixed excange rates (and unwilling to devalue their currencies), had to intervene to protect the value of their currencies in the face of huge monetary movement. Monetary interdependence also resulted in the weakening of national monetary policies of Western economies. For example, the policy of high interest rates, used to curb inflation, was increasingly undermined by capital inflows caused by the very same high interest rate policy.

In spite of its large economy relative to those of Europe and Japan, this monetary interdependence also affected the USA. The overvalued American dollar discouraged American exports and encouraged imports and capital outflows. In 1971 the USA balance of trade deficit soared and for the first time in the twentieth century the USA recorded a balance of trade deficit. In the same year President Nixon announced, without consulting the IMF, that the American dollar would no longer be convertible into gold.

Throughout 1971 there were a series of negotiations among the Group of Ten and the US to find a way out of the crisis. The negotiations resulted in the so-called Smithsonian Agreement of December 1971. This Agreement restored fixed exchange rates, but currencies were allowed to float with a margin of plus or minus 2.25% (which was twice the range allowed by the Bretton Woods Agreement). America agreed to devalue the dollar while Europe promised not to drift into protectionism.

The Smithsonian Agreement was short-lived. Continuous capital movement led to new pressure on the Smithsonian rates and a new currency crisis developed. The situation could not even be rescued by a second 10% devaluation of the American dollar in 1973. Consequently, the system of fixed exchange rates collapsed and developed countries began to float their exchange rates. Floating rates were in flagrant violation of the provisions of the Funds's Articles and in particular Article IV concerning par values and exchange stability. Yet this did not raise any protest from the Fund. Instead the Fund was given the task of legitimizing floating exchange rates according to the wishes of the Western countries.

Thus, the very foundations of the Bretton Woods system have been demolished by Western countries. The IMF and its rules have, since that date, lost their legitimacy. It is, therefore, irrelevant to argue that some (or even all) of the elements of AAF-SAP are in conflict with the IMF Articles of Agreement or IMF policies.

D. ON THE QUESTION OF DOMINANCE

At present, the IMF system is functioning not by virtue of its legitimacy but by virtue of its dominance; the dominance that the IMF derives directly from the economic (and hence political) power of the few countries controlling it. In African, as well as other Third World countries, foreign dominance is manifested in the state of dependent and unequal development which is engineered and maintained by the debt-dependency syndrome. Apparently, it is this aspect that presents the real challenge to AAF-SAP.

The challenge to AAF-SAP comes as a result of the fact that, the majority of the policy measures prescribed by it seem to require either additional foreign exchange (at least for the "take off stage") and/or radical political decisions that might necessitate a change in political power. These constraints are, in fact, closely interrelated with each other and with IMF interventions through maintaining the debt-dependency cycle. That is, the foreign exchange constraint may hinder the making of political decisions necessary for the adoption of AAF-SAP, or may work to strangulate and revoke them after they were made. To illustrate, consider the following two scenarios:

The "Stick" Scenario

A government of an African country undertakes economic reforms that involve measures which are not popular to its creditors. This country will face retaliatory actions in the form of capital flight and drying up of capital inflow. In the case where foreign investments are concentrated in the export sector (which is often the case), with the bulk of their production shipped to their parent companies in the form of exports, foreign retaliatory actions might be enforced by parent companies deliberately boycotting the products of their subsidiaries. The result would be a drop in the demand for the exports of the country concerned, thereby reducing economic activity in the export sector. The country, being historically dependent on foreign investment and foreign capital, would then find itself in a foreign exchange crisis. Using the IMF terminology, the balance of payments deficit which was "viable" and "sustainable" would no longer be so, simply because foreigners had curtailed their aid.

This, together with the consequent slow-down in economic activity in the other sectors of the economy, would increase unemployment and reduce government revenue while at the same time generating social and political pressures for greater government spending.

As the economic situation worsened, with foreign creditors tightening the screw on the government, the exchange constraint would become acute and the country would have no option but to call in the IMF. Having accepted the IMF intervention, the government would not only reverse but also discredit the process of reform it initiated.

The drying up of capital inflows, the flight of capital, and the drop in exports would provide the IMF technical diagnosis with the evidence of an overvalued exchange rate, and lack of confidence in the country's currency. Hence devaluation would be prescribed as a remedy. The slow down of economic activity would provide the evidence of "distortion" in the market forces. The widening government deficits would be viewed as the result of government pricing and subsidization policies. In short, the Fund technical diagnosis would observe the effects rather than the real causes of the aggravated economic situation (Hussain 1983).

If the country proved to be obedient to the IMF, the Fund would convene a debt rescheduling conference and mobilize rescue aid for the troubled country, thereby making it even more dependent on foreign aid than before. The IMF programme would result in a large reduction in real incomes and wages. As a consequence the government would lose popularity while social and political pressure for a change of government would increase. A new government would come into power (in some cases through a military coup) (Payer 1974). The new government would promise radical social and economic changes. Capital inflow could dry up, capital leave the country, and so on.

The "Carrot" Scenario

A government of an African country may draw a socio-economic plan aiming at achieving a measure of independent and equal development. But the implementation of some of the projects in the plan might require addditional foreign exchange. The government approaches foreign donors to secure the foreign exchange component . However, because of the aid consortium technique the types of loans which the country receives are either tied by explicit stipulation of where they may be spent (and in some cases subject to further limitation with respect to the types of goods which may be purchased), or tied to projects initiated by lending sources rather than projects initiated by the country's planning body. This state of affairs is enforced by the activities of the "Commission Mafia" making foreign borrowing a hysterical process. "Anyone can go to the President with a project... tell him it is a good idea and get his go-ahead for it" (Financial Times 5.9.1979).

As a result, the guidelines for economic development outlined by the Plan become impossible to follow. The initial plan has to be modified to incorporate projects in the field of transportation and services, as dictated by the type of loans received from Western sources, and to make room for projects financed by direct private foreign investment. The result is a collection of different projects that can hardly form an integrated development programme.

This has a profound effect on the distribution of investment expenditure (financed by foreign borrowing) among the various sectors of the economy; with apparent bias towards the sectors which are not directly productive such as the transportation, communication and services. Over the plan period the country continues to draw on foreign loans, mostly from Western sources, to finance its capital goods and other imports.

As foreign debt accumulates, with part of it beginning to fall due for repayment, export earnings must be increased substantially to meet the country's imports and debt repayment bill. But the foreign loans the country has received were not utilized to increase the capacity of the export sector; the economy is still dependent on the export of one or two primary products. The country thus becomes increasingly dependent on additional loans to finance its imports as well as its debt service.

Over time, the foreign exchange position of the country becomes acute and foreign donors refuse to extend additional loans unless the country signs an agreement with the IMF. The Fund steps in and imposes its standard model of devaluation supported by demand management policies, additional aid and debt rescheduling. Over the IMF programme period the country is made more dependent on foreign aid (including food aid) and on the export of traditional primary products, thus enforcing the process of dependent and unequal development... and so on.

Although they appear in abstract form, the two scenarios can be deduced from the recent economic history of some Third World countries that attempted to break away from the vicious cycle of debt and dependency. For example, the "Stick Scenario" typifies the experience of Jamaica during the era of Mr Manley, while the "Carrot Scenario" resembles the experience of Egypt following the death of President Nasser. The exact details of the experience of individual countries may vary, but the end result is the same: from dependency to dependency. This is achieved by strangulating the country through the curtailment of capital, forcing it to leave its independent path, or offering the 'carrot of aid' to drag the country back to the "debt trap". In the past, Third World countries have confronted foreign dominance with some policies of their own. However, we fear that the adoption of the AAF-SAP will be met with the same retaliatory tactics.

E. SOME CONCLUDING REMARKS

There is no doubt that the original IMF policies were essentially designed to serve Western interests and they were, later on, modified for the same purpose. There is also no doubt that the original IMF rules were essentially designed to suit the functioning of Western economies and they were, later on, demolished for the same purpose. What remains of the IMF system is neither legitimate nor appropriate. The issue of legitimacy, as such, can, therefore, be disregarded in any debate on the obstacles to the adoption and implementation of AAF-SAP.

The policies of AAF-SAP are essentially designed to free African countries from their state of dependent and unequal development, maintained by the debt-dependency cycle. An African country that overcomes the political constraint by adopting AAF-SAP, might be confronted with the foreign exchange constraint. This can be "relaxed" by foreign donors extending their conditional aid in a manner that nullifies and reverses the policies of AAF-SAP, or can be tightened by foreign donors forcing the country to retreat from the AAF-SAP path.

A successful implementation of AAF-SAP thus seems to require, among other things, the support of an "independent" source of foreign exchange, a source that extends development credit to needy African countries without conditions save those related to the commitment of the recipient country to AAF-SAP, a source that can be relied on to protect African economies from the retaliatory actions of orthodox donors.

It seems relevant to end this paper by recalling what we have suggested in a previous paper (Hussain 1989). We suggested that no one African country could undertake AAF-SAP single handedly. Yet a group of African countries with a unified stand might succeed. We are of the opinion that the task of taking serious steps towards the implementation of AAF-SAP could be pioneered by a small group of truly African governments who were committed to the cause of the poor majority. This pioneering group could create an African Adjustment Bank with financial, administrative, consultative and executive functions. Such a bank could be endowed with "positive conditionality" geared towards the attainment of adjustment with transformation, regional integration and development. The Bank could solicit financial support from Arab as well as Western donors who wanted to promote mutual economic cooperation (as opposed to economic dominance) with member countries. It might even negotiate directly or indirectly on behalf of member countries with foreign donors and Western "international" organizations.

REFERENCES:

Dorrence, G.S., *Rapid Inflation and International Payments,* Finance and Development Vol. 11. No. 2, June 1965 p.67.

Economic Commission for Africa *Towards a Human-focused Approach to Socioeconomic Recovery and Development in Africa*, The International Conference on the Human Dimension of Africa's Economic Recovery and Development, Khartoum 1988.

The African Framework to Structural Adjustment Programme 1989.

Hussain, M.N. *Studies in the Theory and Practice of IMF Conditionality and Devaluation in Developing Countries*, Ph.D. thesis, University of Kent, 1983.

De-adjustment Mechanisms of IMF Adjustment Programmes, paper presented to Conference on African Alternatives, IFAA-IDS. Tanzania.

Leftinck, P. *Monetary Policy and Structural Adjustment,* Finance and Development Vol 1, No 3 December 1964.

Payer C. *The Debt Trap, the International Monetary Fund and the Third World,* Monthly Review Press, London 1974.

Polak, J.J.*Have Economists said their Final Word in the Fight Against Inflation*?, Finance and Development Vol 5, No. 3 1968.

TOWARDS HUMAN CENTRED DEVELOPMENT

Hassan Sunmonu

Much as one could commend the World Bank for the depth of research devoted to the third chapter of the LTPS, INVESTING IN PEOPLE, there are shortcommings which should be underlined lest African countries again fall into the trap of adopting the policy recommendations of the World Bank wholesale. This chapter would have been more appropriately titled " Human Resource Development and Utilization", though it has nothing to say about how the utilization of the human resources affects development.

Yet it is noteworthy that the World Bank has come to accept at last, though very reluctantly, that development cannot be measured solely in terms of Gross Domestic Product (GDP), Gross National Product (GNP), a healthy balance of payments, etc. It is therefore reassuring to hear the World Bank say in the second paragraph of the chapter that:

> "measuring development in terms of access to basic health services, education and food is more satisfactory than using most other yardsticks". It worked for them to cite the example of Kenya which, "with a GNP of only \$330 per capita has lower infant mortality and higher primary school enrolment rates than say Cote d'Ivoire with a GNP of \$740 per Capita."

Only five years ago the wealth of nations was measured by the size of the GDP, the GNP and a healthy balance of payments (whether it was enough to import for 6 months, 1 year or 3 years). It was not until a year or two ago that certain United Nations agencies started to measure the quality of life as an indication of the wealth of nations. So now no country can embark on meaningful human resource development without, for example, tackling the problem of the eradication of illiteracy, estimated to be in the region of 50% in most African countries.

But this chapter of the LTPS does not make any reference to mass literacy programs and this is one of its shortcomings. With the exceptions of Ethiopia, which reduced illiteracy from 93% to 30% in ten years, and Tanzania, which made incredible inroads on illiteracy with mass literacy campaigns, most sub-Saharan African countries still have very high rates of illiteracy. Human Resource Development addresses the issue of illiteracy. It is very important that African countries embark on mass literacy programs that are well planned, co-ordinated and financed if they are to eradicate illiteracy from the continent by the year 2000. Yet Chapter 3 of the LTPS makes no reference to such programs.

It should be remembered that a high literacy level in countries like Japan and South Korea is one of the major factors in their rapid development. A common feature of "the tigers of Asia" is their high literacy rate and the premium they put on human resource development. We in the trade unions of Africa believe that you cannot talk of Africa catching up with the rest of the world without first talking about eradicating illiteracy

It is amusing to see the World Bank shed crocodile tears over the poor quality and general decline of social services in sub-Saharan Africa since the 1980s. Is not the World Bank or its twin sister the International Monetary Fund (IMF) partly responsible for this decline? Has it forgotten that one of its conditionalities is the withdrawal of subsidies from social services by African countries?

If the World Bank has forgotten, we the workers and the people of Africa have not forgotten. This hypocrisy reminds me of the saying that "Success has many fathers but failure is a lonely orphan". In this report the World Bank does not want to be identified with the failure of the social services on the continent. Instead of saying these failures or non-performance are due to its own policies and those of its twin sister the IMF it gives other curious reasons. That is something we find in this report, the World Bank not having the intellectual honesty to admit that they have played a part in the social decline.

It is this hypocrisy and arrogance that both the IMF and World Bank display in blaming African governments rather than their anti-people policies for the failure of their Structural Adjustment Policies in Africa. No wonder there is not a single success story among the 33 African countries that have adopted their Structural Adjustment Programs.

Until recently the case of Ghana was cited as the success story of IMF Structural Adjustment Programs in Africa. But it was a question of live now and pay later. Structural Adjustment is increasing by geometrical proportions the indebtedness of Ghana.

Among the measures the report says are needed to achieve food security and primary education and health care by the year 2020 is the lowering of fertility rates, since "unregulated population growth" strains the capacity of social services throughout sub-Saharan Africa. "Policies to improve health care have to go hand in hand with those to reduce fertility levels and vice versa."

Why do we say good education, employment opportunities and an improved standard of living are a more important antidote to high population growth?

Take the case of young girls. If they go to school and spend between six and eight years in primary school and then proceed to secondary school and other institutions this will delay their prospects of early marriage. The acquisition of education or a career diminishes their reproductive cycle. This is a natural way of reducing high population growth. When you don't educate and there are no employment opportunities or improvements in the standard of living people *will* reproduce. Employment, education and a higher standard of living are more viable solutions to population growth in Africa than all the measures this report suggests.

This chapter also covers the issue of food security. A recent study makes the point that well co-ordinated plans are needed sub-regionally, nationally and continentally to ensure food self-sufficiency. The study deals at length with the relation between population growth and food security, urging African countries to shift their emphasis from overproduction of cash crops (with resultant low prices) to food production, preservation and processing. That is where we differ from the LTPS . This would not only ensure food security and self-sufficiency but also guarentee employment for millions throughout the continent.

Agricultural research institutes in Africa should double their efforts in high yielding areas and bio-technology to increase continental food production. We, in Africa don't want food security; we want food self-sufficiency. Food security, in the way the World Bank is pushing it, implies Africa would still depend on food strategies that could be replenished by food aid and which actually stunt our efforts at producing food for ourselves, by ourselves.

In the section on education there is an attempt by the LTPS study to limit Africa's objectives when it says:

> "there are two immediate priorities to improve the quality and relevance of education at every level and to re-direct public resources

> towards basic education and health care including, family planning for the longer term. By the year 2020 at the latest, African countries could realistically aim for universal food security, primary education and primary health care"

The Report wants to limit the educational objectives of Africa, even to the year 2020. In order to further discourage expenditure on higher education the study goes on to say:

> "cost-benefit studies in the past decade in 16 African countries estimate the social rate of return for investment in education at 26% for primary, 17% for secondary and 13% for higher education."

The Report is indirectly telling African countries, "Don't bother to invest in higher education when the social return is only 13%. Since the returns for primary education are higher, why not concentrate only on primary and secondary?" This is why I accuse the Report of trying to sabotage African educational objectives and make African countries produce people only just literate enough to be directed. Yet science and technology will determine the course of development and have already started to determine the course of development throughout the world . Any country or continent that does not invest seriously in science and technology will never catch up or make any advancement in the future.

African countries should reject, as we in the trade union movement in Africa reject, these attempts by the World Bank to limit Africa's objectives. These attempts will only compromise the future development of Africa .

In order that Africa does not remain the hewer of wood and drawer of water for the other continents of the world the following steps should be taken:

1. Mass literacy programs for the eradication of illiteracy from the continent by the year 2000. The conception, design, implementation, supervision, management and financing of these programs should involve governments, employers, workers, women, youth, students and grassroots organizations. Ethiopia is a worthy example of how a country, no matter how poor , can mobilize people and organizations to help in mass literacy programs. We are proud of Ethiopia and Tanzania in the succes s of their mass literacy programs.

2. The present education system should be overhauled from primary through secondary to higher education, including the design of

education curricula to emphasize the teaching of science and technology, vocational training, and entrepreneurship with an emphasis on research and management. The present education system in most African countries is still colonially oriented . Pupils and students are trained to look for jobs in the civil service, or white collar jobs in the limited private sector. The public sector is saturated and this is the main reason for the high unemployment. Countries like Britian have started to re-orientate their educational programs to encourage and teach entrepreneurship from primary level. Education should be geared towards actual employment prospects, especially self-employment.

3. Education in Africa should not only be universal but as far as possible free, at least to the secondary level. It should be accessible and affordable for all by the year 2000. It is universally accepted that the best investment is investment in human resources. You can only develop this resource when people are well prepared.

In conclusion, the development of the human and natural resources of Africa for the peace and prosperity of Africans is the sole responsibility of Africans. Africans should not abdicate this great responsibility. The international community and agencies should assist Africa to achieve this objective.

PART TWO

The Uruguay Round of GATT

THE URUGUAY ROUND: THE POLITICAL DIMENSION

Chakravarthi Raghavan

The Uruguay Round was launched in 1986. But there has never been much public debate about it, either in the industrial countries or in the Third World. What little has been published has been in the financial and business pages, mostly representing the views of the trade negotiators of the North. Often presented as negotiations involving international trade, the Uruguay Round, unlike earlier GATT Trade Rounds, is not really about trade. It is in fact about the organisation of the world economy, the economic and social organ isation of countries and international economic relations.

Even though in GATT and the Uruguay Round issues are cloaked in technical and trade jargon or presented as economic mysteries beyond the reality of politics, they are all about economic and social policies and therefore predominantly issues of politics. In one form or another they will affect people's lives and futures, and those of their children and grandchildren, and they ought to be publicly debated before decisions are made, particularly in these days when democracy, democratic participation and decision-making are emphasised.

Discussions and negotiations in the Uruguay Round over the last four years suggest that in most industrial countries, the parts of the governments dealing with 'development' and 'co-operation' do not know what is being done by the parts concerned with 'trade', and the two often work at cross purposes. Even within the European Community (EC) Commission one wonders whether the divisions concerned with Third World Development and Co-operation, Protection of the Environment and Sustainable Development and Promotion of Democracy and Human Rights, are fully aware of what is being done or pushed forward by the EC's External Relations Division (which deals with foreign trade) or Agriculture Division, and whether there is sufficient coordination between the Commissioners for External Relations and Development Cooperation.

Footnote: For example, Claude Cheysson, as Development Commissioner, agreed at UNCTAD-7 that Third World countries should be helped to fight capital flights and dishonest trading practices such as under or over-invoicing and transfer-pricing. At about the same time, the EC negotiators in the Uruguay Round negotiations (at the insistence of their pharmaceutical and chemical enterprises) called for rules under non-tariff measures to prevent pre-shipment inspection agencies (widely used by Third World countries to check on the quality and prices of their imports) from comparing export prices with those in other parts of the world. Such inspections are one way of discovering the illegal remittance of profits, common in the pharmaceutical and chemical trade. Recently the EC compromised and allowed such inspections. But this is just one example of the dichotomy between development co-operation and neo-merchantilist trade practices.

WHY THE TALKS COLLAPSED

When the Ministerial session of the Uruguay Round talks collapsed on the night of December 6th, perhaps it came as a surprise to the public in Brussels and to the EC and its negotiators who are accustomed to cliff-hanging, eyeball to eyeball negotiations, and to reaching compromise agreements at the last minute or after stopping the clock when one side or the other 'blinks' and gives way.

That the Brussels meeting would fail had, however, been evident to any careful observer for some time. The failure had been on the cards since early 1990 when the US and the EEC decided to postpone all substantive negotiations to the very end.

The staging of a crisis at the Brussels meeting to force Ministers to reach compromises when faced with the prospect of failure and the threat of a trade war had been built into the script. The problem was that different people had written different scripts, with varying scenarios for triggering the crisis and resolving it. These scripts got mixed up, the actors began ad-libbing and the stage-managers lost control. As a result the talks were extended for an unspecified 'short period' with a decision that they could be reconvened when appropriate.

Early in 1990, when the dates of the Brussels meeting were set, it had been envisaged that the profile of a global package would be prepared by July. All but a small core of hard political issues were to be resolved in the Geneva negotiations, leaving very few to be decided in Brussels. Despite having agreed to this, the US and EC later decided they could not reveal their cards until the end. Others warned that this was a high-risk strategy but the GATT Secretariat acquiesced.

The result was a bulky 390 page document: "Draft Final Act embodying the results of Uruguay Round of Multilateral Trade Negotiations", a document bristling on every page with square brackets (around disagreements of substance and form) on technical and political issues requiring the Ministers' decisions. With the best will in the world, none of the Ministers, not even the most technically competent among them, was capable of understanding, addressing or making a decision in the short time available.

In the event there were no real multilateral negotiations at Brussels, merely bilateral talks between the US, the EEC and some 'non-transparent', so-called 'green room', consultations; the entire negotiations were held hostage on one issue – agriculture. So everything was sent back to the negotiators in Geneva who had referred it to the Ministers in the first place. They were expected to sort out the issues by early February 1991.

This deadline was set to suit the US administration and the fast-track procedures of the US Congress under which agreements are voted on but not amended. Such a method of negotiating may be acceptable when the issue involved is tariff reductions on imports or concessions on exports but is wholly inappropriate when social and economic policies involving politics and govenance are involved. Public debate and discussion are necessary for the informed consent of the population. Only then would the agreements endure.

WHAT WILL HAPPEN NOW?

GATT Director General, Arthur Dunkel, has now been entrusted with the task of pulling a rabbit out of the hat, by holding consultations and promoting agreement in all areas. However, in reality, any resumption of talks seems to be predicated on US-EC bilateral deals on agriculture, with Dunkel playing the role of broker and persuading the others to accept. It also appears to be predicated on the development of some kind of mini-package with the other parties 'scaling down their ambitions' but providing substantial agreement on intellectual property, investments, services, subsidies, countervailing measures etc., that would be 'acceptable' to the US Congress. In other words, the price of US-EEC agreement on agriculture will be paid by the Third World.

But the gap between the US and the EEC on agriculture is so vast that no acceptable compromise seems to be in sight. Even if they do find a compromise, overall agreement is not certain: the disagreements that led to the collapse of the Round involve many more are as and issues. For example, on Services. Here the US had hoped to establish the 'right of establishment' for its service enterprises in other countries and their 'national treatment' ie. equal treatment with domestic enterprises. This was really a demand for instant liberalization and would have put Third World countries at a serious disadvantage.

But what emerged was not to the liking of the US. Third World countries who were at first reluctant to engage in the service negotiations participated actively and presented a coherent and logical approach that found acceptance, even at the level of the US technical negotiators. A draft framework was evolved that would place Third World countries in a less asymetric position in the negotiations, enabling them to liberalize less than the industrialized countries (ICs); liberalization of domestic regulations on 'establishment', 'market access' and 'national treatment' would be gradual and negotiable. They could trade concessions in some service sectors of benefit to the North in return for concessions of benefit to them.

As this picture emerged, various US service sectors gradually realised that they may lose their advantage and would face competition in the US. Their attitude changed and the US position changed too. Washington pulled the rug out from under its own negotiators. The US resigned from the more than a century-old trade theory of Most Favoured Nation treatment (MFN) to which everyone had agreed and, almost at the end, proposed conditional MFN and derogations in sectors where the US may not be at an advantage.

At Brussels, seemingly, the US indicated it would compromise on this issue. But when one examines the US compromise talk closely it can be seen for what it is – a different form of conditional MFN. The US said it would agree to MFN provided the initial offers (for liberalization, national treatment, etc.) of all signatories, including major Third World countries, were 'substantial' and acceptable to the US.

MAJOR DIFFERENCES PERSIST

Other major North-North and North-South differences remain on Anti-dumping and Subsidies, Investment Measures, Intellectual Property Rights, Textiles, Safeguards, etc. On Subsidies, for example, there are differences between the US and the EC and between both of them and the Third World. Third World countries are asked to enter into commitments to completely phase out subsidies on production and exports of their industrial products –

subsidies that they can ill afford but which they are forced to grant to enable their exporters to overcome market imperfections – while ICs do not envisage eliminating or phasing out subsidies on primary products.

It is sound economics that market imperfections are often best corrected through state intervention and the provision of subsidies, and that under-developed countries, trying to diversify and industrialise, have to provide subsidies to encourage industries to export. But the draft text of this envisages Third World countries foregoing their right to provide subsidies and, in a relatively short span of time, phasing out existing ones. The 'graduation' concept in the draft subsidies agreement, based on per capita incomes, for example, will require Gabon, an under-developed economy dependent on a one-commodity export, oil, where annual per capita incomes gyrate according to fluctuations in oil prices, to undertake the same obligations as the major industrialised countries as of now and phase out all subsidies on industries, thus preventing them from promoting diversification of the economy.

In the entire negotiations, the ICs are telling the Third World to adopt so-called 'market' policies – but as preached rather than as practised by the ICs themselves. For example, Third World countries are asked to eschew the very policies that the ICs adopted in the past to attain their present stage of industrialisation and development – whether it be in relation to investment policies, intellectual property protection or other matters of state intervention and support.

Given the differences amongst the major trading partners and between them and the major Third World economies, it is difficult to envisage a major package of agreements embracing Agriculture, TRIPS, TRIMS, Services and Textiles being concluded in the immediate future. All the scenarios for 'success' seem to be predicated on a mini-package that is sufficiently attractive to command US Congressional support and enable its adoption under fast-track procedures.

The mini-package would apparently include measures to institutionalise GATT in the form of a new Multilateral Trade Organisation (MTO). There is much talk of 'scaling down' ambitions on agriculture, textiles etc., but no sign of scaling down the ambitions of the ICs in the new themes or their demands on the Third World.

At another level, it seems that those who helped to launch the Round in 1986 did so on assumptions that are no longer valid, and hence they are no longer serious about the outcome. The US administration and the EC Commission launched the Round and brought in others by holding out some carrots and sticks (the threat of withdrawing market access rights). But while they were trying to negotiate with each other they were also trying to use it to further their domestic agendas. For instance the US administration probably wanted to get its ideas (Reaganomics) into both the Uruguay Round Agreement and to change relations between the White House and Congress as well as between Washington and the States. The EC Commission bureaucracy also had in mind the vision of a post-1992 European single market and was trying to use the Round to prevail over member states on trade and non-trade matters.

Developments since 1986 have, however, changed the situation. The US has now become the world's biggest debtor and dependent on foreign savings. It is also losing the edge in several service and technology areas. With other disputes between the White House and Congress, the trade issue has probably become a lesser priority.

Developments in Eastern Europe have changed the priorities of the EC Commission which probably now thinks it would be better off by first creating a Single Market and using this to make others comply with its rules.

Who then is really interested in or pushing for agreement in the new Round? It is the TNCs who now operate and trade globally and want the same rules and rights in all countries, enabling them to operate worldwide without any interference in their operations by host countries. In number the TNCs are only 20% of the world's enterprises trading internationally but they account for nearly 80% of trade in goods and services.

Perhaps there is something to be said for their aims. There is nothing wrong in their seeking level playing fields around the world with clear rules on their rights. But every right should carry an obligation and if there are to be internationally laid down rights surely there should also be clearly laid down obligations for TNCs, and for the governments in their home countries which champion them.

GATT AND THE ENVIRONMENT

Dr Mohamed Suliman

As a student of the environmental sciences I came to know of the Uruguay Round of GATT almost by accident. Driven by the curiosity of the layman and assisted by the diligent efforts of "GATTics" like C.Raghavan, Martin Khor and others, I gradually began to understand some of the immense implications of the new GATT agreement especially for Third World countries. No-one can fail to recognize the historical parallels and similarities between the classic colonization crusades of the last century and the badly disguised attempts to re-colonize the Third World, through a new international trade agreement. History is repeating itself not as farce, but as tragedy.

Everyone is coming to recognize that international trade, producing and exchanging goods and services among nations, is a very complex process in which economic, social, cultural and even future considerations, intertwine. And people *are* trying to challenge this very complexity. Now, suddenly, the idle stick of GATT is thrown into the arena and turns into a huge snake that devours all the smaller snakes, the World Bank and IMF included, and, behold, the world is miraculously a simple and one dimensional entity. This one dimensional entity is called Free Trade.

The Uruguay Round of GATT does three things:

1. It ignores certain important issues.

2. It smuggles in non-trade or quasi-trade issues.

3. It seeks to police the world.

Firstly, it seeks to ignore the right of developing countries, the so-called Development Principle, which gives developing countries certain exemptions and privileges in order to develop their weak economies. It also ignores the increasingly recognized concept of Sustainable Development, which takes environmental considerations into account. And it totally ignores all social and cultural issues pertaining to international trade.

Secondly, it smuggles in non-trade and quasi-trade issues like Trade Related Investment Measures (TRIMS), Intellectual Property Rights (TRIPS) and Services. And, thirdly, it seeks to police the world through the harmonization or liberalization of all trade, the imposition of "Cross Retaliation" measures and the founding of an overpowering international trade organization.

By ignoring the issues of major concern to Third World countries: the deteriorating terms of trade, debt and the right to development, the Uruguay Round of GATT is gradually and systematically trying to implement and legalize the hegemony of the developed industrial countries over the world.

In developing and developed countries ordinary people will benefit from fair trade that caters for environmental concerns, but free trade that covers agriculture, TRIPs, TRIMs, and services, imposed by "Cross Retaliation" actions and by an overpowering international trade organisation can only promote the interests of the TNCs at the cost of the people, their environment, health, safety and future. Not only in developing countries but also in developed countries,

> "the result is ever expanding monopoly powers over ever extending geographical areas in more and more economic sectors, controlled by fewer and fewer mega-companies. The reverse side of this coin is increasing erosion of Third World countries' control over the national economies to foreign enterprises and their increasing marginalization in the world trade."

(Martin Khor, Third World Economic Sovereignty at Stake in the Uruguay Round, Third World Network).

THE ENVIRONMENTAL IMPLICATIONS

The basic objective of the Uruguay Round of GATT is the liberalization of international trade, which, in economic terms, means free markets or laissez-faire practices. This is an antithesis of the concept of sustainable development, which incorporates economic developement, environmental protection and people's needs, today and in the future.

It is alarming that an international trade agreement which regulates about 80% of the $3 trillion annual global trade, does not include protection of the environment in its guiding principles, but relegates it to the "exceptions" to the general agreement. At the time when "Green" pressure is at last imposing some restrictions on the unscrupulous practices of the World Bank and the IMF, the TNCs are trying to evade any environmental obligations through the Uruguay Round. Even where a country's legislature recognizes the need for environmental protection this could soon be superceded by an international GATT agreement altering national laws of signatory countries to make them consistent with GATT: the "Harmonization Principle".

HARMONISATION

If the Harmonization Principle was imposed on world trade, international standards would be higher than those prevailing in Third World countries. In the absence of the development principle there would be no time frame for Third World countries to catch up with changing standards, hence this Principle would be an additional and perhaps insurmountable barrier for goods from the Third World to developed countries.

The US Government made a proposal at the Uruguay Round to harmonise international food safety standards. The intention was to eliminate 'protectionist' environmental standards by allowing international bodies such as the FAO-affiliated Commission on Codex Alimentarius to establish standards on food safety. If the United States GATT proposal is accepted, then countries which totally prohibit DDT in food will have to accept this lower standard. A country like Holland or a state like California will have to curb their environmental laws. The TNCs attack is directed not only against the Third World, but also against advanced countries and states. It seeks to weaken the democratic process in developed countries and take decision-making powers away from elected governments.

ELIMINATION OF IMPORT AND EXPORT CONTROLS

The liberalisation drive in the Uruguay Round of GATT could lead to the elimination of import and export restrictions. If this proposal succeeds then the whole world market will be open to the TNCs . Any attempt to curb trade in favour of the environment, e.g. bans on the export of raw timber, could be considered illegal and could lead to retaliation measures.

Some may argue that there would be room within the new GATT for environmental protection measures if these could be proven scientifically. Scientific proof is costly in time and money and when reached is not always conclusive and certainly not binding on wealthy countries unless they choose it to be so. A case in point is the reaction of the U.S. administration to the call to restrict emissions of greenhouse gases. In spite of all the scientific evidence the Bush administration has refused to take any action because the case against greenhouse gases is not scientifically rigorous!

INTELLECTUAL PROPERTY 'RIGHTS' (TRIPS)

Trade-related intellectual property rights have been included in the new themes in the Uruguay Round of GATT. Industrialised countries insist on the harmonisation of these laws, i.e. that all countries adopt their TRIPS. TRIPS are protectionist measures which tend to slow the transfer of technology and knowledge, thus constituting a barrier to knowledge.

When the industrial countries were developing their economies, they had weak patent laws, but now they insist on enhanced, rigorous, uniform laws on intellectual property rights (not privileges as this should rightly be). In the TRIPS there is no mechanism for recognising and determining the value of the genetic and biological material obtained from Third World countries. The TNCs take the genetic material freely and sell us the hybrid dearly, and, in addition they demand laws to protect their rights and rentier income for their intellectual input.

Liberalisation of trade and protectionism of intellectual property seem to be antitheses, yet the TNCs choose to mix them. A member of the U.S. Senate, John Heinz, is a witness to the dichotomy inherent in the Uruguay Round. In his letter dated 31 July 1990, to Carla Hills, the U.S. Trade Representative, he wrote:

> "It is also apparent that the current GATT instruments, such as article XX, exceptions for measures designed to protect human, animal or plant life or health, were drafted at a time when environmental issues were not considered entirely relevant to the trade debate. These provisions, and the GATT instruments as a whole, therefore, do not provide an adequate basis for dealing with the new laws, regulations, and international agreements that will emerge in today's environmentally conscious world."

SUSTAINABLE DEVELOPMENT WINS THE BATTLES BUT LOSES THE WAR

The ecology movement in developed and developing countries, supported by the WCED Report, "Our Common Future", have been winning many battles in national and international arenas. The concept of sustainable development is being endorsed everywhere, except in GATT. The new GATT would override all national and international commitments pertaining to sustainable development. Is the new GATT ordained to absolve the TNCs from the 'sins' of sustainable development?

ARTICLE XX - GENERAL EXCEPTIONS

As mentioned earlier, the draftees of GATT relegated all environmental considerations to Article XX (General Exceptions) which provides that "nothing in this agreement shall be construed to prevent the adoption or enforcement by any contracting party of measures... (b) necessary to protect human, animal or plant life or health...a measure seeking the shelter of Article XX must satisfy two considerations:

i. It should not be applied in a manner which would constitute a means of arbitrary or unjustifiable discrimination between countries where the same considerations prevail.

ii. It should not be a disguised restriction on international trade.

Environmental considerations are exceptions to the General Rules of GATT and the conditions set on an exception are also subject to interpretation by the leading industrialised nations, as experience has amply shown. The working group on environmental measures and international trade was set up within GATT in November 1971. It never met. Only recently has Austria, on behalf of the European Free Trade Association (EFTA) proposed that the GATT Council convene the working group, twenty years on.

GATT is not serious about the environment. Free trade is the only overriding principle. A penetrating example is the decision concerning the export of domestically prohibited goods. In 1982 a Ministerial meeting decided that GATT members "shall to the maximum extent feasible, notify GATT of any goods produced and exported by them but banned by their national authorities for sale on their domestic markets on grounds of human health and safety." Only notification is urged for poisonous products banned in the producing country solely on the grounds of human health, not the health of the whole environment!

Seven years later, in 1989, GATT council established a Working Group to consider the need for new measures to regulate export of nationally banned dangerous chemicals. The following year the Chairman of the Group announced that members were considering a draft decision on products banned or severely restricted in the domestic market. However, one member reserved its position and the deadline had to be extended to 1991. It has taken a whole decade to deal with the restricting of exports of poisonous products to the Third World by industrialised countries, where these products were banned! More intricate measures will take decades to resolve.

Third World countries should insist on the fundamental restructuring of the Uruguay Round and of GATT itself. This is in the interests of the people in developing and developed countries. The environment should be a fundamental principle of national and international trade, not an exception to the general principles.

THIRD WORLD ECONOMIC SOVEREIGNTY AT STAKE:
The Uruguay Round

Martin Khor Kok Peng - Third World Network

Part I: BACKGROUND TO URUGUAY ROUND

Trade representatives of industrialised countries attempted a little-known but extremely dangerous assault on the economic sovereignty of Third World countries through the Uruguay Round talks under the auspices of the General Agreement on Trade and Tariffs. These developments received scant public attention because the negotiations were conducted behind closed doors and remained hidden from the scrutiny of citizen's groups, legislatures and governments.

Many Third World governments involved in the negotiations increasingly expressed unhappiness and frustration at the attempts by the major industrial countries to bulldoze through proposals to drastically alter the rules of international trade and economy. They were severely hampered by lack of technical and diplomatic clout and co-ordination among themselves, but increasingly took combined negotiating positions. The Uruguay Round in particular and GATT, in general, have become by far the most important arena of North-South economic negotiations. The industrialised countries attempted thorough the Round, to extend and tighten their control of the world economy in general as well as over the national economies of Third World countries. They sought, in many areas of negotiations, to downgrade or remove entirely the "development principle" which had hitherto been accepted within GATT rules.

According to this principle, developing countries can be granted exemptions or privileges (such as a longer time frame) to comply with certain GATT obligations in recognition of the difficulties they face in building-up their long-term development capacity. In other words, the 'free trade' promoted by GATT is tempered with the 'development principle'.

In the Uruguay Round negotiations, this principle was increasingly eroded and ignored by the major industrial countries which sought that Third World countries be treated no differently from themselves. The industrial countries also showed less interest in giving concessions in areas of particular interest to the Third World, for instance reducing tariffs on their products or improving access for its products to the industrial countries' markets.

Instead, the real focus of the industrial countries' Uruguay Round was to radically restructure GATT itself and immensely enlarge its powers so that it became a "world economic policeman" empowered to enforce new rules that maximised the unimpeded operations of transnational corporations. The principle of "free trade" (the absence of state interference, intervention or controls) was sought by the industrial countries to apply internationally – not only in the traditional GATT area of goods but also in the areas of services and investment flows. Present restrictions and obligations imposed by Third World govenments on foreign companies seeking to relate to or set up bases in their countries were portrayed as going against "free trade".

The transnational companies want the removal of barriers to their unimpeded activity, so that they can penetrate Third World economies more effectively. As an effective and well organised lobby they enlisted their govenments to make use of the Uruguay Round to extend the "free trade" principle from merely trade in manufactured goods to the "new themes" of services, investments and intellectual property rights.

If these new areas are incorporated into the GATT framework in the way proposed by the industrialised countries, Third World countries will have to "liberalise" or open up their national economies. This will allow transnational companies to have sweeping rights not only to export to the Third World, but to invest and set up bases in Third World countries, and to be treated like locally-owned companies, with hardly any state controls over them. This "freedom" will be granted not only in manufacturing and agriculture but also in the service sectors (such as banking, insurance, transport communications, media and professional services).

But the TNCs and the industrial countries wanted to have their cake and eat it too. They also proposed that GATT become the policeman to enforce new regimes on "intellectual property rights" that would oblige Third World countries to have national laws granting patent rights and protection to TNCs for their products and technologies. This would severely hamper the possibility of Third World companies or agencies developing their own technological capacity, and would grant monopoly power over technology to the TNCs.

This goes against the principle of "free trade" which the industrial countries are using as an argument to pry open the Third World.

This contradiction exposes the double standards that underlie the industrial countries' self-interest in pushing for the adoption of "new themes" or new powers to GATT. They use liberalism or free trade as an intellectual weapon to push for the liberalisation of services and investment flows to the Third World; but simultaneously they want to restrict the free flow of the technological capacity of the Third World by imposing patent obligations and intellectual property rights regimes onto the Third World.

Behind all the pseudo-scientific arguments about free trade is stark and simple fact, that the industrial countries were using the Uruguay Round to enable their TNCs to greatly expand their monopoly powers over all possible areas and levers of the world economy and national economies. Through the incorporation of services and investments into GATT-like regimes, the TNCs would be able to penetrate sectors and areas in the Thrid World in which presently the locally-owned small and medium sized firms (or family-owned, so-called informal sector) predominate. It needs little imagination to foresee that these smaller local economic units would be swallowed up rapidly when the TNCs entered the scene.

And by instituting intellectual property rights laws to protect the monopoly position of TNCs, the national companies of the Third World would be prevented from developing their own technologies and thus constituting a future threat to the existing TNCs.

Thus the industrial countries' corporations would expand and extend their monopoly powers in trade and investment in all sectors and in all areas of the world (not only the Third World but, with the collapse of Eastern Europe and the USSR, also the former socialist countries), whilst at the same time instituting monopoly rights over technology so as to prevent the emergence or development of possible competitors. The "newly industrialising countries" (like South Korea and Taiwan) would be kept in check whilst potentially powerful Third World contenders like India, Brazil or China would find it difficult to make an "economic take-off".

The result would be expanding monopoly powers over ever extending geographical areas in more and more economic sectors controlled by fewer and fewer mega-companies. The facilitation of this ever increasing concentration of capital and market power is what was being sought from the Uruguay Round. The reverse side of this coin was the increasing erosion of Third World countries' control over their economies to foreign enterprises, and their increasing marginalisation in the world economy.

THE ROLE OF TNCs

The role of TNCs in influencing the Uruguay Round became increasingly clear. The United States administration, the main proponent of the "new themes", worked closely with US companies. In 1982 the US first expressed the need to apply GATT principles to trade in services. It was motivated by the desire of US service companies to expand their markets and operations and thus to break down barriers, especially in the Third World, that hindered such expansion.

Representatives of TNCs regularly lobbied in Geneva when negotiations were in progress. The effectiveness and scale of such lobbying became evident in July 1990, during the Group of Seven industrial countries' leader' summit in Houston, when the Uruguay Round figured prominently on the agenda.

In May 1990 leading US companies and business organisations announced the formation of a high-powered "MTN (Multilateral Trade Negotiations) Coalition". Chaired by the former US Trade Representative, William Brock, now in private business, the group included American Express, General Motors, IBM, General Electric, Cargill, Citicorp, Procter & Gamble and other companies; as well as the US Council for International Business, American Business Conference, National Association of Manufacturers, Coalition of Service Industries, International Investment Alliance and Intellectual Property Committee.

The Coalition described its aim as follows: "The MTN Coalition is a broad alliance of American private sector interests committed to a strengthened and more effective multilateral trading system. The Coalition includes an array of business, farm, consumer and trade associations which have joined with many others in an education and mobilisation campaign in support of comprehensive multilateral trade a greements in the current negotiating round of GATT... The MTN Coalition will build public support for Congressional implementing legislation if the agreement is satisfactory".

At the July 1990 Houston Summit the MTN Coalition organised a high-powered press briefing and released a summary report of an "Eminent Persons

Group on World Trade" underscoring the links between the two. Brock said he found it "incredible" that the G7 countries were unable to negotiate seriously, especially on agriculture, whilst the stakes in the Uruguay Round were so high. He said that, while the Summit's focus was on farm reforms, "yet agriculture is not the issue... Rather it is the lynch pin to agreement on issues of greater magnitude, issues that really matter, like intellectual property protection, services, investments and subsidies."

This clearly indicates that to the business sector the new themes were the real agenda in the Uruguay Round. The President of the American Business Conference, Barry Rogstad, said US businessmen saw a strengthened GATT as the "single best way to create an environment to expand their international success".

The business lobby's effectiveness, at least where the US was concerned, was shown by the top priority that US President Bush gave to the Uruguay Round at the G7 Summit. The US Agriculture Secretary Clayton Yeuter stressed that "a successful end to the Uruguay Round negotiations is ten times more important to the US than good relations with the Soviet Union". In the summit's final communique, the G7 leaders described the Uruguay Round as having "the highest priority on the international economic agenda" and they pledged "a high level of personal involvement to exercise the political leadership necessary" to ensure the Round's success.

Part II: THE NEW THEMES AS MECHANISMS TO DOMINATE THE THIRD WORLD

a) Services

In most Third World countries, the service sectors are the last remaining areas to be still under local control, since imported manufactured products have increasingly taken over the market of locally-made goods. Many Third World countries, to protect domestic services, have laws restricting the entry or the operations of foreign service enterprises in areas like finance, media and communications, transport and professional and business services.

In the developed countries, services form the fastest-growing sector, having overtaken manufacturing. Service companies want access to the relatively protected Third World market and thus want the barriers to be broken down.

The US proposed that services be included in discussions on the reform of GATT but due to objections from many Third World countries the services discussion was conducted separately from other GATT issues with the aim of formulating the framework of a "General Agreement on Trade in Services" (GATS). Nevertheless it was part and parcel of the Uruguay Round talks and the US wanted it to eventually be incorporated into GATT as it proposed that the GATT secretariat should also be the secretariat for GATS.

The arguments used by the US and other industrial countries, and the mechanisms they suggested to open up the Third World's services market were as follows:

- Free trade in goods (the traditional area of GATT's jurisdiction) is by itself inadequate since services are now important. So we must extend the free trade concept from goods to services.
- But unlike goods one cannot export a service to another country unless the service provider (person or firm) is itself present in the importing country. Thus to facilitate free trade in services, there must be freedom not only in trade in services but also in investment. Service companies must be given right of establishment in other countries. In other words, if a bank or legal firm wants to set up a branch in a Third World country, that country's government must grant it the right to do so.
- However, if the foreign company is discriminated against vis-a-vis local companies (for instance, local firms are granted preferential treatment), that is said to be a distortion of the free play of market forces. So the Third World government must grant treatment to foreign firms, i.e. treat them with the same conditions as one would treat local companies.
- If a country violates the above principles, for example by not allowing an American bank to open, then the country of the offended company (in this case the US) can retaliate by forbidding the offending country's banks from opening in its country.
- But that is not all. If services are eventually incorporated into GATT in a super trade regime or organisation, then the violating country could face cross retaliation actions. This means that the offended country can retaliate not only against the offending country's banks but also against its products. For instance that country's rubber, copper or textiles may face increased import duties or even a ban. This will of course be a more potent threat than merely retaliating against a Third World country's banks or other service companies which have very little business in the industrial countries and would thus not be significantly affected by any retaliatory moves.

It is this possibility of cross retaliation (to link action in one area of trade or business to retaliation in another category of product, service or business altogether) that invests the GATT framework with so much power and "bite". In most other international economic fora, if countries do not in practice follow what they have committed themselves to through resolutions, there is little possibility of acting effectively against them. But the threat of retaliation and cross-retaliation is a strong mechanism that may be used to enforce commitments taken by countries, especially those countries with little economic clout.

If the above principles and mechanisms are pushed through, then it is only a matter of time before the TNCs assume control over the wide range of service activities in Third World countries.

In the first half of 1990 there was a major development in the services negotiations when two separate groupings of Third World countries put forward their own proposals for a services framework. In February 1990, a group of 11 Latin American and Caribbean countries (Brazil, Chile, Colombia, Cuba, Honduras, Jamaica, Nicaragua, Mexico, Peru, Trinidad, Tobago and Uruguay) sponsored proposals.

This was followed in May 1990 by another draft agreement on services tabled by seven African and Asian countries (Cameroon, China, Egypt, India, Kenya, Nigeria and Tanzania). In the two Third World texts, the offer to liberalise the Third World's service sectors gradually is balanced by the right of the Third World countries to have policies in accordance with national priorities and development needs.

In general, the Third World position on services includes the following principles:

- Trade in services is defined to cover transactions involving cross-border movement of services, consumers and factors of production provided they are for specific purposes and of limited duration. This definition rules out rights of "permanent establishment", "foreign direct investment" or "international immigration" that are demanded by the industrial countries.
- Whilst Third World countres are committed to 'progressive liberalisation', this would be subject to national policies and laws (which shall be respected) and full account should be taken of their development situation and needs. In particular, the principle of relative reciprocity should apply; Third World countries should not be required to make concessions that are inconsistent with their development needs. Individual Third World coun-

tries should have flexibility for opening fewer types of services in line with their development situation. Priority should also be given to liberalising sectors of interest to the Third World and to measures that facilitate access to their exports.

- The increasing participation of Third World countries in world trade and the expansion of their service exports must be promoted. They should be allowed to strengthen their domestic services capacity by providing incentives or by taking steps to secure a minimum level of domestic production or other measures.
- Third World countries should be allowed to impose conditions on foreign service suppliers or companies, such as limiting the type of commercial presence; requiring training and employment of local people; imposing surcharges and different tax rates; requiring a minimum level of local content in operations; requiring firms to provide access to technology and information on global business operations.
- Given the above two principles, 'national treatment' (giving foreign firms the same rights as local firms) would not be automatically granted.
- Each country should take measures to ensure that service suppliers do not engage in unfair practices, acquire undue market domination or obstruct competition.
- Any services agreement should have its own regulatory institution (e.g. an International Trade in Services Organisation) which would be seperate from GATT. This is important so as to prevent the threat of cross-retaliation between services and goods.
- Countries can exempt certain services from the agreement on the grounds of protecting public morals, cultural and social values, safety and health, national security, environment and the development of Third World countries.
- Third World countries can also apply safeguard measures (to withdraw or modify their concessions) to enable correction of balance-of-payments deficits; to remedy unforeseen negative effects from liberalisation commitments; when there is a need to promote certain service sectors; to correct problems caused by technological changes; or to deal with adverse trade effects caused by concentration of ownership, market domination and restrictive business practices.

The principles above would provide a certain degree of protection to Third World countries from being otherwise overwhelmed by the full blast of opening up to foreign service companies. However, the proposals of the Third World are not acceptable to the industrial countries which are demanding full liberalisation from the Third World.

b) Investment and TRIMS

In another area of the Uruguay Round negotiations, the developed countries have been advocating that rules regulating "Trade-Related Investment Measures" (TRIMs) be introduced into GATT. At present most Third World governments impose certain conditions on foreign investors as a requirement for their establishment.

Among these "investment measures" are:

- Local content requirements (the foreign company must use a specified minimum ratio of local materials in its production);
- Export requirements (obliging an investor to export a fixed percentage of production);
- Trade-balancing requirements (restraining an investor from importing more than an equivalent amount or some proportion of exports);
- Local equity requirements (specifying that a certain percentage of the company's equity be held by local investors);
- Limitation on remittances of profits and other foreign exchange restrictions; and
- Manufacturing limitations (reserving certain markets to local firms to protect them from being eliminated by foreign competition).

Third World governments argue that these measures are needed to protect their countries' balance of payments positions, to prevent unethical TNC practices such as transfer pricing or monopolistic market allocation, to ensure the survival and development of local firms, or to put a limit on TNC ownership of key sectors. Such conditions are imposed not to restrict "trade" as such but to enable the development of local industries or to ensure a certain degree of economic sovereignty or to counter restrictive business practices of the TNCs.

The developed countries, however, want the Third World to remove most existing TRIMs. They argue that these TRIMs distort free trade because they have an influence over conditions of production and thus over costs and prices. They also insist on 'national treatment' (that foreign investors be treated the same as local investors).

Whilst Third World countries are willing to negotiate on the trade-distortive effects of investment measures, the industrial countries want to prohibit the measures themselves. If the US proposals are accepted, Third World govenments would no longer be able to require foreign firms to have local equity participation or to transfer technology, to have local content in its output or to limit foreign exchange outflows.

The rights of the foreign investor are also to be safeguarded by providing that the government of the investor's home country can take up the purported violation with the host govenment. Failing a satisfactory outcome, the company's government can retaliate against the trade and property of the host country. Thus the right to retaliation will give 'bite' and ensure enforcement of the foreign investor's right.

Moreover, the proposals would enable cross-linkages and retaliation, enabling the home countries of foreign investors to retaliate against the goods exported by an offending Third World country.

The EEC and Nordic countries take the argument even a step further, by proposing that the removal of restrictions on investments be applied not only to foreign investors but also to domestic investments. They argue that since any investment measure could have a trade-distorting effect (and affect trade of other countries in third markets) the GATT rules should apply to both foreign and domestic investments. Since local investors may be unable to defend themselves against their governments' regulations, the GATT regime should make all offending measures "GATT illegal". A foreign government could even intervene on behalf of a local company against its own government if it were to raise a complaint about being affected by a TRIM.

These proposals go far beyond the curbing of distortive effects on trade in goods, and far beyond the present GATT mandate. They amount to the establishment of a fully-fledged system to regulate both foreign and domestic investments, to spell out and enforce the right of investors by forbidding governments from imposing many existing conditions and restrictions on investors.

According to C. Raghavan, a senior Indian journalist and GATT observer in Geneva: "The scope and sweep of the US proposals go even beyond the claimed property rights of foreigners, rights backed by gunboat diplomacy and military occupation, that prevailed in the colonial era, and now sought to be reinstated and backed by trade sanctions" (South-North Development Monitor 1 February 1990). In this envisaged new investment system, GATT is seen to be the world policing agency.

These proposals are being fought by Third World countries. In March 1990, a group of 14 Third World countries (including Argentina, Brazil, China, Cameroon, Egypt, India, Nigeria, Tanzania and Yugoslavia) submitted their own proposals, opposing the use of the Uruguay Round to create rights for investors or to prohibit investment measures. Instead, the negotiations should be confined to tackling adverse trade effects of investment measures within the existing GATT framework.

They argued that investment measures were used by governments to fulfill social and development objectives and to counter corporate behaviour that threatened these objectives. Investment measures such as local equity, remittance and other foreign exchange restrictions, technology transfer and licensing, were used to promote development and had no impact on trade. Some other measures, though trade-related, did not significantly affect trade or the trade effects were beneficial to Third World countries and thus justified on development considerations.

The 14 countries stated that the clear intention of the Uruguay Round mandate was to focus on the trade restrictive and distorting effects of investment measures – and not to establish an international investment regime nor to circumscribe the capacity of governments to employ investment measures per se.

Investment measures were used to fulfill social and economic policy objectives. Thus the countries rejected any a priori presumption that investment measures were inherently trade restrictive and distorting. If it could be shown that an investment measure had a direct, significant adverse trade effect, a clear causal link would have to be established between the measure and the alleged effect. If such a link was established, then "appropriate ways would have to be found to deal with the adverse effects, and not the measures themselves".

The countries argued that investment measures were legitimately and justifiably used by the Third World to promote development, enhance employment and also to offset trade restrictive and distorting effects of corporate practices. They defended the use of many investment measures which the industrial countries are seeking to outlaw, for example:

- Local content requirements are important to encourage the use of locally available inputs and promote local industrialisation; as well as to prevent foreign firms from importing parts from their parent companies even if comparable local inputs were available.
- Domestic sales requirements (obliging foreign firms to sell in the local market) were intended to ensure that some products were available locally in sufficient quantity and at appropriate prices.
- Local equity requirements were aimed at ensuring a degree of control for local mangement, encouraging local savings and technology transfer, and for national security reasons.
- Remittance and other exchange restrictions were used to reduce balance of payments pressures on host countries.
- Export requirements were also used to improve a host country's foreign exchange position and to counter the possibility of foreign firms blocking exports due to international market allocation strategies.

The Third World viewpoint is that the prohibition of such investment measures would be tantamount to establishing a world investment regime that granted tremendous freedoms to TNCs whilst prohibiting governments from taking legitimate measures to protect their countries from unethical corporate practices or to promoting the growth of locally-controlled economic activites. Any country that broke the new laws would face retaliatory sanctions. This tremendous widening of the powers of GATT is unacceptable to the Third World .

Although the Third World views were submitted to the chairman of the TRIMs negotiating group at his request, Third World delegates were greatly disappointed when in May 1990 he presented a draft text of an agreement on an international investment regime that reflected the viewpoints of the US, Japan, and the EEC whilst completely ignoring their viewpoints and their official submissions.

c) Intellectual Property

On the insistence of the industrial countries, "Trade-related intellectual property rights" (TRIPs) was also included as a "new theme" in the Uruguay

Round. Although there were other fora (such as WIPO and UNCTAD) that had for many years dealt with the subject, the industrial countries insisted that the issue be dealt with under GATT to enable cross retaliation. A Third World country agreeing to a TRIPs agreement but not adhering to it could in future find trade sanctions imposed against its export goods.

"Intellectual property" refers to a design, technology or product invented by a person or corporation and "rights" refers to a recognition that the inventor should be granted a reward such as the exclusive right to use it or to earn royalties by renting out its use. Such "rights" are conferred by awarding patents, copyright, or trademarks to the "owner" or inventor.

The industrial countries argue that such rights and rewards must be conferred to provide incentives for research, development and innovation. Through the Uruguay Round they wanted all countries to adopt intellectual property laws like their own, thereby having one standard set of such laws, to be administered and enforced by GATT.

Among the elements of their proposals were that:

- Intellectual property rights laws should be uniform for all countries and the present laws in the industrial countries should be taken as the standard;
- These rights would be enhanced where the majority of Third World countries were concerned since these countries presently conferred less rights than did the industrial countries;
- The enhanced rights for intellectual property owners need not be counter-balanced by obligations imposed by society or governments upon them;
- These rights should be given in almost all types of products. On patents, the US position was that there be no exclusions given; whilst the EEC would allow exceptions for inventions contrary to morality or public order and for plant and animal varieties and biological processes for plant and animal production; and Japan would allow exclusion for inventions contrary to public morality, order to health and those manufactured through nuclear transformation;
- The rights should be granted for relatively longer periods than prevailed in most Third World countries. The US proposal was that copyright protection be for at least 50 years and patents for at least 20 years;
- Intellectual property rights fell under GATT jurisdiction because they had an effect on trade. Thus GATT was a competent body to administer them;

- Once TRIPs was accepted within the GATT umbrella, countries allegedly not following the provision would face retaliation and cross-retaliation, thus giving "bite" to the agreement.

The Third World position is opposed to the above. Its stand is that the recognition given to an inventor is more of a "privilege" than a "right". The benefits given to the individual or company for the invention must be balanced by the public good or the public's right to benefit from technological innovation or knowledge. Without such a counter-balance, the intellectual property privileges granted to the inventor would become purely monopoly rights to collect rentier income. In effect they constitute a form of protectionism, the protection of the inventor's benefits, which curbs the diffusion of technology or knowledge and thus prevents technological development.

This protectionism ran directly counter to the principle of liberalisation that the industrial countries were advocationg so piously in other areas of GATT negotiations. Thus there were double standards in the industrial world's approach: liberalisation if it suits us, protectionism too if that suits us; the real underlying principle is pure self-interest.

The kind of intellectual property regime proposed in TRIPs would effectively prevent the diffusion of technology to the Third World, and would tremendously increase monopoly royalties of the TNCs whilst curbing the potential development of local Third World technology. At present only one per cent of patents worldwide is owned by Third World persons or companies. In the 1970s, only 200,000 patents (out of 3.5 million worldwide) were granted by Third World countries and 84% of these were owned by foreigners. Yet less than 5% of the foreign-owned patents were used in production in the Third World.

The TNCs register patents in the Third World not to operate their technology there, but to prevent others (especially locals) from copying or using their technology, thus protecting the Third World market for sales of their products produced in the North. Patent protection is thus used as a major mechanism to perpetuate or even enhance the monopoly position of TNCs by preventing others from emerging as contenders.

Indeed when the industrial countries themselves were developing their economies, they had weak patent laws, thus enabling their own local technological growth. Now they have reached high-tech status they impose strict patent regimes and want the Third World to do likewise. Being already in an extremely dependent position technologically, the Third World would become totally marginalised if the industrial countries' TRIPs proposals prevailed.

At a Third World Patent Convention in New Delhi in March 1990 organised by citizen groups and attended by 94 participants from 14 countries, a declaration was drawn up expressing deep concern at the "grave threat posed by the TRIPs negotiations to the inalienable rights of our countries to design and operate national intellectual property regimes, corresponding to our national genius and serving our national interests. There is no connection between intellectual property and trade. GATT is not the proper forum in which the question of intellectual property rights should be negotiated".

In May 1990, a group of 14 Third World countries including Argentina, Brazil, Chile, China, Colombia, Cuba, Egypt, India, Nigeria, Peru, Tanzania and Uruguay presented a draft agreement on TRIPs at the Uruguay Round negotiations which was basically opposed to the industrial countries' proposals. The essential elements of their position were as follows:

- Recognition of the sovereignty and autonomy of countries to determine the areas of patentability, the period and conditions of patent protection. This is counter to the idea of one set of uniform laws;
- Governments' right to grant compulsory licenses is specifically recognised. Compulsory licensing allows the government to force a patent or copyright holder to forgo its monopoly and allow the government or others to use the invention. This can be done on grounds of public interest or in the event the holder abuses the patent;
- An intellectual property regime should balance the rights granted to owners with obligations by them. The rights include: preventing others from working the patented product or process; assigning the patent and concluding license contracts; receiving 'reasonable remuneration' if a government uses the patent or grants a compulsory license. The obligations of a patent owner include: disclosing the invention in clear and complete manner; giving information concerning corresponding foreign application and grants; working the patent invention in the country where the patent is granted within fixed time limits; in respect of license contracts, refraining from abusive or anti-competitive practices adversely affecting technology transfer;
- In the event of non-fulfilment of obligations, national laws can provide for remedies against the patent holder. These include the granting of compulsory license in case the patent holder does not work the patent or in case

of abusive or anti-competitive practices of the holder; cancellation of registration if a trademark is not effectively used; annulment of contract in case a holder engages in practices that violate regulations on competition and technology transfer.

- The following areas can be excluded from patent protection: inventions whose use would be contrary to public order, morality and health; plant and animal varieties or biological processes for producing plants or animals; discoveries and materials already existing in nature; medical treatment for humans and animals; nuclear and fissionable material.

Besides the above points in the Third World group's draft agreement, several Third World delegations also made clear that any TRIPs accord could neither be located in GATT nor linked to the GATT system of rights and obligations (South-North Development Monitor, 7 April 1990).

When the Third World group put forward their proposals at GATT in May 1990, the industrial countries rejected them. "With varying nuances, they made clear that they would not even consider (the draft agreement) as a basis for negotiations and indirectly warned that unless Third World countries agreed to accept enhanced GATT standards and rules, unilateral retaliation against their trade would follow." (C. Raghavan, South-North Development Monitor, 18 May 1990). At present the North and South countries are still far from agreement in the TRIPs negotiations.

Part III: THE URUGUAY ROUND AS BATTLEGROUND: NATIONAL SOVEREIGNTY VERSUS TNC WORLD POWER

At the week-long session of negotiations at Geneva at the end of July 1990, the Third World delegations were acutely frustrated by the unwillingness of the industrial countries to carry on any substantive discussions because they had not yet sorted out disagreements among themselves.

At the end of the sessions, the Brazilian ambassador Rubens Ricupero issued a statement on behalf of Third World delegations concluding as follows: "Developing countries wish to reaffirm their readiness to negotiate constructively... (but) will reject any attempt to impose upon them a pre-negotiated package agreed only by a few. It is with profound concern that developing countries find themselves compelled to declare that, if the current situation is not changed soon, the Uruguay Round will be in serious jeopardy as a result of the lack of political will of the major participants".

At present, the stakes are still heavily stacked against the Third World as the industrial countries are well organised and are basically in control of the levers and processes of the negotiations. If the proposals of the industrial countries win the day, then governments would cede a large part of their countries' sovereign right to regulate their own economies, environment, health and even culture. This right would be ceded to the companies which would be granted freedom from interference or intervention by nation states.

National laws of all signatory countries would have to be altered to make them consistent with the international GATT agreements. These laws might be in areas as diverse as finance, equity ownership, services, intellectual property, environment, health, culture and media. The legislatures of these countries are not adequately aware (many are not even aware at all) that many of the important national laws they have passed should be superceded by international agreements which their countries' diplomats and trade representatives are negotiating. Worse still, many governments (especially in the Third World) do not realise the full import of what their representatives are negotiating. Many Third World countries have only weak delegations at the United Nations in Geneva and they have to cover not only GATT but other agencies such as WHO and ILO. Very few of them were able to follow the complex negotiations taking place in the many committees and the issues of the Uruguay Round, let alone make meaningful representations. Both at the negotiating centre in Geneva as well as in the capital cities, governments, legislatures, interest groups and citizen groups were not able to recognise the full implications of the Uruguay Round.

There are now two major but contradictory trends in the world. On one hand we have the "Green Wave", a rapidly increasing realisation amongst both public and governments that unchecked and uncontrolled operations of companies and the economy are leading to catastrophic environmental and health effects. Toxic chemicals and products, toxic wastes, nuclear power, industrial pollution, acid rain, deforestation, wasteful energy use, increasing carbon dioxide in the atmosphere, the Greenhouse Effect and ozone depletion are the result of too much freedom given to economic forces, especially the big companies. As a result of growing ecological and health consciousness, there is a growing trend of legislatures and governments acting to control the operations and effects of companies, of economic projects and industrial plants.

This trend extends beyond national boundaries: there is realisation of the need for regional and international cooperation and agreements on the international trade in hazardous products and wastes, on global deforestation, climatic change, ozone layer depletion and the Greenhouse Effect. There is increasing awareness of unethical corporate practices and corporate crime (including insider trading, financial fraud, the falsification of safety test results, the knowing sale of toxic products and the illegal dumping of wastes) and the need to tighten regulations and controls to prevent such corporate practices.

For the past two decades at least, Third World countries have also been attempting to improve their position vis-a-vis transnational companies through the (so far unseccessful) negotiations at UNCTAD and in other fora for codes of conduct on transnational corporation behaviour and for reforming existing intellectual propoerty laws in favour of Third World interests.

The Third World has also tried to stabilise its commodity export position and terms of trade through commodity agreements and schemes, but these efforts suffered a major setback when the industrial countries pulled out of most of the schemes in the second half of the 1980s.

As against the "Green Wave" (which calls for more effective regulation to monitor and check the behaviour of companies), there has emerged a powerful trend which advocates the granting of untrammelled and unchecked freedom for "market forces" to dominate economic and other spheres of life. Under the banner of "free market, free trade, deregulation, privatisation and liberalisation", this trend or ideology calls for maximising freedoms and resources to be given to companies to operate, whilst minimising the role of governments either to participate in economic activity or to regulate the behaviour and effects of the companies.

The companies' battle for the "free market, deregulation and privatisation" started at the national level and, having been relatively successful there, is now attempting to extend it to the international level with the concept of "free trade".The chosen arena for this ambitious project is precisely GATT and the vehicle is of course the Uruguay Round. If the industrial countries' proposals, (especially for the "new themes") succeed, then almost the whole world's market would be open to the TNCs for investment and services besides the traditional area of goods; and moreover, the companies' monopoly over technology and production processes would be ensured.

It is thus no wonder that the "MTN Coalition" of big business and the US administration consider the new themes in the Uruguay Round to be of maximum priority; to the extent that a "successful conclusion" of the Round would be considered "ten times more important than good relations with the Soviet Union".

For the Third World (as well as those who care about the environment, health and culture), "free trade" or "liberalisation" cannot be taken as good or a goal in itself. Free trade is not necessarily a good thing, contrary to what the industrial countries' ideologists and trade representatives would have everyone believe. Between two equal partners or contenders, free trade may bring mutually satisfying, fair and equitable benefits. But if one party is far stronger than the other, the benefits are likely to be unequally shared; indeed the weak party may not gain at all but instead suffer losses.

In the case of international trade in goods, services and investments, it could well be that in the context of liberalisation and "free trade", the TNCs would take over control of many sectors and areas of the national economies of the Third World whilst the locally-owned industries, trades and services would be increasingly marginalised and prevented from developing.

To use a sports analogy, putting the Third World and the industrial countries on equal footing in "free trade" would be like pitting a malnutritioned African child against Carl Lewis in a 100 metres race. The rules are the same for both: they can start only when the gun is fired, they both have to run 100 metres, and the first person to breast the tape wins. This would be a "free" race in that the rules are similar for every participant but it certainly would not be considered a "fair" race since the contenders are not of equal capacity to begin with.

Similarly, to insist that Third World and industrial countries alike be subjected to the same rules (no tariffs, no national laws hindering foreign investments in goods or services, the same patent laws) might be defined as "free trade" but would not constitute "fair trade".

What the Third World should be fighting for is fair trade, not free trade. What it desperately needs is an international economic order that recognises and caters to its development needs – the need to produce to satisfy the basic human requirements of its people, the need for greater social equity, and ecologically harmonious forms of development. For such an economic order to evolve, the North must recognise that it owes a great historical debt to the South for the centuries of exploitation and transfer of resources (human, financial and natural) that have left the Third World so far behind economically that it cannot compete on equal terms.

That is why Third World countries consider "the development principle" such a crucial concept. It recognises that being in a weaker position (due to historical reasons) the countries of the South are entitled to exemptions and privileges in GATT obligations, and that they are entitled to consider their development needs as top priority when negotiating the terms of agreement in various areas of the Round. Unfortunately even this "development principle", which has till now been accepted within the GATT framework, is under full-scale attack by the industrial countries. If this assault succeeds, the Third World will have almost nothing left with which to defend itself in the vicious terrain of the international economic arena.

The Uruguay Round can be seen as the TNC Empire's grand way of striking back at the Green Wave and at the Third World's emerging demands for global economic justice (as epitomised by calls for a new international economic order). The first trend (advocating urgent governmental and inter-governmental interventions to save the world's environment through greater controls over companies; and advocating a fair deal for the Third World in a more equitable world economic order) is now clashing head-on with the second trend (which is vigorously pushing for liberalisation on global scale with the removal of controls over TNC behaviour).

With the present balance of forces, the advocates of the liberalisation trend appear far more powerful and they may succeed in pulling off a virtual coup, going over the heads of national legislatures to secure greater freedoms and powers for themselves in international law. On the other hand the advocates for a future that is environmentally sound and that allocates a fair share of global resources to the Third World, have a cause that has far more attraction and staying power.

How the battle of the trends is resolved may well determine the shape not only of the world economy but of the world for many decades to come.

PART THREE
The Fraser Report on Africa's Commodity Problems

TOWARDS A SOLUTION TO AFRICA'S COMMODITY PROBLEMS: A COMMENT

S. Tomori

INTRODUCTION

Bearing in mind Africa's high dependence on commodities in terms of exports, imports and production, the United Nations set up an Expert Group in 1989 with rather grandiose terms of reference: "to examine the nature and causes of Africa's commodity problems and to make recommendations on national, regional and international measures for revitalization and diversification of Africa's commodity economy."

The result is AFRICA'S COMMODITY PROBLEMS: TOWARDS A SOLUTION, a compendious and somewhat pretentious report.

The report places Africa's commodity problems at the doorstep of both external and internal factors. The principal external factor is unstable commodity prices in the international commodity markets, a phenomenon always reflected in unfavourable terms of trade. However, the report argues that Africa's commodity problems cannot be attributed mainly to external factors because countries in other regions with similar problems have progressed while Africa has lagged behind. The main culprits for Africa's commodity problems , the report posits, include:

> "ill-advised government policies, unenlightened administration and organisation, a serious lack of agricultural scientists and extension officers, a poor knowledge of international markets, a lack of investment in transport and other infrastructure essential to effective competative production and an economic policy framework which offers overseas investors few incentives" (p28)

MAIN RECOMMENDATIONS

The report thus submits that the solution to these problems lies primarily with African countries and people. However, it does not fail to recognise the crucial role the international community will play in fostering an external environment conducive to getting the region's economies out of the doldrums. It argues vigorously for a commodity strategy which entails:

> "a conscious upgrading of the importance of the Commodities Sector within the planning, budgeting and policy formulation of individual African countries. Such an upgrading requires...a co-ordinated and internally consistent package of mutually reinforcing policies and measures relating to the Commodity Sector and its roles in overall development programming".(p36)

Lack of a clearly focussed commodity strategy is given as a reason for the failure of previous actions aimed at revitalizing the commodity sector. The report calls for a commodity strategy which will revolve around three elements:

i) A change of attitude,

ii) Organisational reform, and

iii) Resource mobilisation.

Various recommendations are put forward. The report argues for the creation of a follow-up mechanism to ensure that its recommendations are carried out to the letter. Key United Nations agencies and organisations are to be used, with the UNDP assuming responsibility for co-ordinating the activities of other agencies and for monitoring progress.

The report, as rightly pointed out by Ismail-Sabri Abdalla, an Egyptian member of the Expert Group, "is an act of faith in the market forces" - a faith which is misplaced. A prima facie case has not been established for the inherent superiority of market forces over regulation. There is not a single industrial country that did not employ vigorous protection at some stage of its history. Even the miracle economy of the century, Japan, continues to protect its industrial development in a variety of ways. While Japan is under immense pressure to relax some of these regulations, the lesson we have learnt is that proper regulation, far from being a constraint to growth, can be an indispensible tool for achieving rapid economic development.

AN ASSESSMENT OF THE RECOMMENDATIONS

The implicit assumption in the report that the international commodity market is highly competitive is disturbing. It betrays an acute ignorance of the functioning of the international commodity market. Any keen observer knows that the market is rigged against producers. It is a buyers' market. The market complexities are not fully captured by the standard demand and supply tool and the assumption of instantaneous market equilibrium. The real market does not consist of large numbers of consumer nations bidding against one another competitively for Africa's commodities, but rather of a handful of powerful multinational trading corporations. Such a market setting can definitely not be regarded as competitive .

In addition, the report's submission that the commodity sector be given the highest priority in national plans confirms the comparative-cost-advantage approach to development – an approach which has been discredited by Africa's development record of the past. The adoption of a Commodity Strategy, which all the recommendations revolve around, is, to say the least, risky. Undue reliance on the Commodity Sector will only exacerbate the regions vulnerability to changing commodity prices, for what looms up over the horizon is "market failure". The bargaining power of African economies in the international market place is weak and there are no indications that commodity prices will stabilize. The claim that the economic reform programmes embarked upon by African governments in the early and mid-1980s are "now beginning to provide a context in which growth and adjustment can reinforce each other,"(p3) is not convincing. Similarly, the assertion that African countries which adopted reforms endorsed by the World Bank and the IMF are doing better than those that did not, cannot be substantiated. A similar claim by the World Bank in 1989 was discredited by facts provided by the ECA. Is it financial help or reform which is responsible for the "miracle"? And why have these better policies and the generous financial help not brought far bigger benefits to the reformers?

Moreover, some of the recommendations in the report are contradictory. In one breath, it calls for the continuation of IMF/World Bank sponsored SAPs (which in the name of "rationalising" government expenditure have reduced budgetary allocations to social services, notably education and health) and in another, it calls for heavy investment in human capital - education. According to this report, the success of the Commodity Strategy hinges critically on an educated populace. What a contradiction!

The report stops only a shade short of asking Africans to hand over their functions of policy formulation and implementation to groups of "experts" from the IMF, World Bank and United Nations organisations such as UNCTAD, UNIDO and UNDP. Here again it betrays acute ignorance of our past developmental strategies which foundered on the rocks of foreign "experts" advice. The recommendations of the Group will only lead to the loss of economic independence.

Its appeal to developed countries to offer a supportive environment in terms of opening their markets to commodities from Africa and providing financial resources on concessional terms, will obviously not be needed. To the extent that similar appeals have been made in the past and have fallen on deaf ears, this seems an exercise in futility. The expectation that developed countries will abandon protectionism is illusory – the failure of the recent Brussels talks to reach a consensus on farm subsidies illustrates this.

Overall, the report offers nothing new. It is a rehash of development strategies that have failed in the past, an aggregation of elements of development thinking which have already been discredited. Nevertheless, the authors have made a concerted effort to get to grips with this difficult subject. They did not quite pull it off. The significance of the report lies in its having reawakened us to the need to find solutions to Africa's economic problems. Unfortunately it will go the way of previous studies on the subject and gather dust on the shelves.

THE FRASER REPORT AND THE OAU POSITION

A.A.Dirar

The background to the Fraser Report is that the assembly of Heads of State of the OAU asked the U.N. Secretary General to establish a group of experts to look at Africa's commodity problems. Consequently, the African group in New York asked the U.N. General Assembly to adopt a resolution to that effect. When the group of experts was established its terms of reference were jointly drawn up by the OAU, the UN, the ECA and UNCTAD.

The major shortcoming of the report, in our view, is that it did not address faithfully its terms of references.

Following the publication of the report, African governments meeting in Addis Ababa in August 1990 instructed the joint secretariat to examine the report. What follows is a summary of the common position reached on the Fraser Report.

African governments and peoples pinned a lot of hope on the outcome of the group of experts work. To demonstrate its keen interest and commitment to assist the group in its work, the OAU instructed the Permanent Steering Committee of the OAU to prepare a memorandum embodying Africa's views and recommendations for submission to the group. The Council of Ministers of the OAU in its fiftiest session adopted that memorandom and asked the PSC to present it to the group of experts. This was done during the group's second meeting in Addis Ababa in July 1989. The OAU summit further instructed the Secretariat to monitor closely the work of the group. Indeed the Joint Secretariat of the OAU and the ECA attended all the groups meetings and kept the PSC informed.

It is against the background of the detailed terms of reference provided by the Secretary General that the Joint Secretariat considered the report of the the group of experts on Africa's commodity problems.

Africa has always maintained and continues to maintain, that Africa's development is the responsibility of its peoples and Governments. The African submission to the U.N. special session on Africa, the implementation of Structural Adjustment Programs by most African governments, numerous meetings and the adoption of AAF-SAP and, last but not least, the adoption of the Declaration on Africa's response to changes taking place in the world by the assembly of Heads of State of the OAU, all testify to our unrelenting commitment to do everything within our power to address the economic and social situation in our countries.

We have maintained all along that our efforts have to be supported by international co-operation to ease the burden of adjustment on our people and to accelerate the process of transformation of our economies. We maintain that the international community have to take concerted action to address the issue of export earnings from our commodities together with the issues of the excruciating debt burden and the need for enhanced financial resources.

Africa views the earnings from the export of its commodities as the cornerstone of recovery and development. The continued decline in earnings from commodities and the annual frustrations have made Africa's recovery very difficult. This is further aggravated by the heavy debt service burden which is beyond Africa's capacity to pay and a decline in real terms of net flows. It is ironic that at the time when our economies are in dire need of financial resources, our continent is a net transferrer of such resources to the developed world and international financial institutions.

In the light of its terms of reference and Africa's own memorandum, we expected that the group of experts would make an in-depth analysis of the problems facing commodities and submit proposals which would carry further agreements reached in different international fora and come up with new ones to further the interests of African countries enabling them to overcome the crisis.

We wish, however, to indicate that the report addressed more than two thirds of its recommendations to our governments and only a third to the international community, including the IMF, the World Bank and the UN system. Most of the recommendations addressed to our governments dealt with general economic issues that we exposed as far back as 1986, when we made our submission to the U.N. special session. It was our hope that the group would address its terms of reference instead of opting for a report, and I quote, "which is mainly orientated towards improvements in management and organization."

The group claimed that many of the solutions to the problems of Africa's commodities were known and for that reason it did not consider it wise to expend its effort on them. In the same vein it could be argued that the policy package the group spent so much time on has been exhausted by the World Bank, the ECA and African governments themselves. The group could have done Africa and the international community a service if it had looked into those known solutions to the African commodity problem, analysed them, found out why they were not implemented and submitted proposals for their implementation.

The problems of the declining revenue and fluctuations remain, however. With respect to the former, the group seemed to link this to the decline in Africa's market share. In our view this is not supported by statistics for the volume of commodity exports. The group should have tried to separate the decline in volume of specific exports from the decline in earnings as a result of falling prices, in order that the magnitude of the problem could be clearly seen and recommendations made to address it.

The recent experience of Uganda, which had a bumper crop of coffee in 1989 and ended up by losing $200 million demonstrates our point. The report has not focused on issues in its terms of reference, particularly the immediate and essential problem of commodity price instability. Africa expected the group to address this in detail. Such an analysis could have considered the contingency compensatory financing facility, for example, and made proposals for its improvement.

Instead the group opted to repeat the arguments of the U.N. Secretary General Advisory Group on Financial Flows and more or less repeated that groups recommendations on a matter at the heart of its terms of reference. Other instruments relating to commodities were completely ignored. Market access issues were taken by the group to mean the weak representation of Africa and its weak negotiating capacity. One would have expected the group to come up with proposals, even in this area, which would enable African countries to negotiate market access issues directly with partners concerned.

The question of long term supply and demand for Africa's commodities was addressed in a general manner by the group, irrespective of the supply and demand situations of individual commodities. The group could have provided guidelines for African countries to plan and direct their efforts to specific markets for certain commodities. Instead it assessed that, "Real growth opportunities exist in primary commodity production and trade." Such a sweeping statement could lead to disastrous consequences if African countries invested in a commodity just to discover that such an opportunity no longer existed. Prudent commodity by commodity analysis would have been helpful for African countries to act upon.

With respect to diversification, to which we devoted a large part of the memorandum submitted to the group, we wish to express our surprise that the group did not take on our specific proposals and instead opted for a general statement on diversification that will not further the interests of African countries. It is our firm belief that VERTICAL as well as HORIZONTAL diversification are the pillars of any strategy to revitalize Africa's commodity sector. But most types of diversification would require the full co-operation of the international community through fiscal and other measures to encourage relocation in Africa and industrial processing of Africa's raw materials. These would have to be supported by financial measures such as the Common Front and the establishment of an African commodities processing facility or an African Commodity Front within the African Development Bank. We recommend this in our memorandum.

We also regret the fact that our other proposals in this area such as the African Investment Commission and the African Investment Facility, two instruments we proposed to promote private investment, were not considered by the group.

Likewise the group's recommendations with respect to regional co-operation lacked specificity and settled for the safe assertion of the importance of regional co-operation. No account was taken of the efforts made by African countries and some agencies of the U.N. in this direction.

With respect to the all important area of resources to implement the program, the group adopted a very shy approach, accepting the estimation of the World Bank for the resources required, namely, those estimated for the implementation of the Bank's own report: Sub-Saharan Africa: From Crisis to Sustainable Growth (LTPS). The problem with this is that, firstly, the resources estimated in that report addressed the financial needs of sub- Saharan Africa, which by definition excludes North Africa. Secondly, the resources were to address the requirements identified in that report, which did not include specific measures on commodities. Thirdly, the group itself suggests that measures, particularly Structural Adjustment measures promoted by the Bank, need to be improved. But their shyness extended to the re-affirmation by developed countries of such steps as the commitment to providing 0.7% of their GNP as foreign aid. By contrast, such shyness is not expressed when the group recommends that Africa should immediately cut its defence spending to raise $3.7 billion. While we do not disagree with this recommendation, we would like to have seen a degree of even-handedness in a parallel recommendation to developed countries to cut their defence spending, as requested by the numerous U.N. resolutions, and devote a very small fraction of this to Africa's development.

We are gravely concerned that the report has introduced even more conditionalities for African countries to meet before being eligible for assistance. We note that these are over and above the Bank and the Fund conditionalities:

Firstly, the report proposes a 50% defense cut. Secondly, it recommends that resources for commodity assistance be conditional and only granted to "African governments that have initiated programs of the kind considered necessary in this report."

We have consistantly rejected all conditionalities. It is only natural that we express our strongest opposition to this approach adopted by the group. We have tried to indicate some of our areas of disagreement and disappoinment. The issue is of crucial importance to us and we had very high hopes of the group. We have deliberately left aside issues on which we agree, particularly the issue of food security and collective food self-sufficiency.

We firmly believe nevertheless, that the report provides a start, imperfect and incomplete as it may be. The commodity issue is of crucial importance not only for our development but for our very survival. We therefore call upon the international community to seek ways and means of addressing the problem of Africa's commodities.

While the proposal for follow-up machinery may help to develop commodity strategies if the specialized agencies of the U.N., such as the ECA, FAO and UNCTAD were to play a leading role, we believe this machinery is not equipped to deal with the external factors facing Africa's commodities. While the UNDP is equipped to coordinate activities at the African country level, it is not in our view equipped to deal with other aspects of the commodity issue.

We therefore propose the establishment of a task force of the U.N. Secretary General in which are represented major decision makers in the area of commodities in developed countries and their economic groupings, the executives of the inter-governmental organizations dealing with commodities and African countries. This task force would carry the work of the group a step further by taking into consideration the critical appraisal of the Report by the OAU.

COMMENTS ON THE FRASER REPORT

Bade Onimode

What I intend to do with respect to the Fraser Report is to support the Common Position of the OAU and in the process help to explain and disseminate this position. I want to address four main areas of the Fraser Report:

1. Its approach .
2. The Commodity Strategy.
3. Regional action, that is, cooperation and integration.
4. Action by the international community.

1. Its approach

There are three elements to the approach of the authors of the Fraser Report: attitude, organisational change and resources (pages 37-49). The question is, are these all the elements there should be to a report on Africa's commodity problems? Don't we have objectives?

I wish to argue that it is precisely because the committee did not take cognizance of the importance of Africa's international objectives in commodity trade that these recommendations have become a rehash of the World Bank's LTPS. This is a lazy work and these are an extremely conservative set of recommendations that are largely irrelevant to the current aspirations and strategies of African countries.

On the question – why the failures? (pages 27-36), the report maintains that the causes of Africa's international trade failure are internal. That is clearly false, and we don't have to be professionals to see it. The following questions need to be answered:

i) Is the collapse of international commodity agreements the fault of African countries?

ii) Are protectionist policies, especially in the U.S. since the Reagan administration, an African problem?

iii) Synthetic substitution for raw materials, that goes under the name of bio-technology, has been reducing the demand for raw materials and therefore for Africa's commodities. This is clearly not an African problem.

iv) The rise in prices of Africa's imports has taken place side by side with rising interest rates since the Reagan administration. This cannot be blamed on Africa.

v) Since the 1970s Africa has been suffering from a combination of falling export prices and rising import prices, producing sharply falling Terms of Trade (the ratio of export and import prices). None of this is an internal problem of Africa.

The implication of the Report is that Africans have been lazy, and have not produced enough exports. The Ivory Coast doubled the quantity of their cocoa exports in 1989-90 yet their export earnings fell by over 50%. Uganda had the same experience with coffee.

This suggestion of internal causes for the failures has been copied straight from the LTPS, which concludes that all the causes of the crisis are internal. Then, on page 29, the report makes the statement that, "global consumption of almost all Africa's commodities has continued to rise"

2. Commodity Strategy

I want to address three aspects of this. The Macro-economic, food security and food aid and diversification. Firstly, the macro-economic strategy in effect recommends that African countries should continue to implement World Bank and IMF Structural Adjustment Programs, but that these should be "better phased and implemented...They should be well funded and move towards greater regional cooperation and protection for the poor."(pages 55 and 60-71).The implication is that the committee agrees with the World Bank on the continued relevance of Structural Adjustment Programs that have produced such catastrophic consequences all over Africa. Either the committee does not want to be taken seriously, or it must be mis-reading of the situation on the ground.

Another aspect of the macro-economic strategy is the call for an international commodity strategy. This will involve the IMF, World Bank, and all sorts of international organizations. The question is whether Africa should surrender its sovereignty over international trade to these organizations. This is an aspect of the LTPS recommendation for a global coalition for Africa: that Africa's long term development strategy should be surrendered to a global coalition and largely become a joint enterprise between our governments and these foreign bodies.

The second commodity strategy recommended by the Report is that food aid should be part of a fully integrated package. Food security can be achieved through domestic production, supplemented by imports of food and food aid. But if African countries are facing serious shortages of foreign exchange, how will they pay for the food imports? Secondly, food aid has been used as a weapon of international politics. The case of India is still fresh in our minds. How can we rely on voluntary food aid to assure the security of Africa? The Lagos Plan of Action and other OAU and ECA positions have rejected the notion of food security and insist on national and regional food self-sufficiency. There is a crucial difference between the two. Yet I don't see food self-sufficiency mentioned in this Report.

Food security for Africa must be based on domestic food production and the exchange of food between food-surplus and food-deficit countries in Africa, in other words increased inter-African trade, that is Africa's official position.

On diversification , the commodity strategy recommended by this report is based firmly on the Structural Adjustment Programs that have failed on the ground. It is also based on food aid, which is a fundamental subversion of Africa's commitment to self-reliance. This is why the absence of policy objectives in the report is a problem. Africa's commodity trade is designed to achieve regional and collective self-reliance. But because the committee did not take cognisance of this it recommended what is virtually an externally dependant commodity strategy for Africa. I think I should emphasize that, essentially, what this report is saying is that Africa should continue to promote the same old traditional commodities that we promoted in the 1960s which led to the present problem. So, we are being invited to promote a course of action that generated the problem, while hoping that this same problem will become its own solution. That appears to be a bit metaphysical.

3. Regional Action

On the question of regional action, that is regional co-operation in trade and integration (pages 73-77), the Report calls for better and larger inter-Africa trade as well as better export and payment facilities. But better cooperation and integration in the area of trade is not just the matter of better trade and payments. Inter-African trade and co-operation has been undermined by the existing Structural Adjustment Programs. Why? – because African co-operation and integration depend on harmonization of policies among African countries, joint planning and greater reliance on African resources. The Structural Adjustment Programs treat African countries one by one. Therefore they remove the very basis for African co-operation. Structural readjustment says countries should stand on their own and, in the process, SAP policies make it difficult to harmonize policies among African countries. For example, competitive currency devaluation is one of the major policy instruments in the current SAP programs. In all regions where countries are devaluing their currencies heavily it becomes difficult to promote the harmonization of foreign exchange policies.

Also in the area of agricultural commodities, when you insist that the market impulse should be encouraged and you open up agricultural trade to private stimulators, how can governments plan together? When you insist on market incentives, where does planning fit in and how can various parts of the world engage in closer co-operation without planning at some point? The recommendation for closer African co-operation in this report is contradicted by the recommendation for the continued reliance on SAPs.

The second area of omission in the section on regional action has to do with cooperation in the area of production. I think the OAU and ECA have made it abundantly clear that one of the major barriers to closer African trade, to larger inter-African trade, is the fact that there is very limited African co-operation in the area of production. How can you trade what you have not produced? Most of our countries are engaging in trade but there is very little to exchange. There is very limited production capacity.

In line with the World Bank's LTPS "Strategic Agenda for the 1990s", this report calls for the closer integration of markets in Africa. The implication is that, since African countries are not co-operating in production and are producing what they don't consume and consuming what they don't produce, it will be easier for advanced countries to trade in Africa. With the removal of trade barriers the trans-national corporations will be able to flood our markets with their commodities. We have nothing to sell so it is they who will benefit. We reject this.

One major pillar of African integration from our point of view is cooperation in production. This requires the pooling of limited resources of capital, technology and skilled manpower so that African countries can undertake joint multi-national projects in the production of hydro-electricity, in agriculture, in industry. Because of fragmented markets in African countries many of the industries required will not get the total co-operation of individual African countries. For example, in 1980 we undertook to study the production of electrical models and accessories in Europe. At the headquarters of Phillips we were told that a modern factory producing electrical accessories could satisfy the entire demand of the Nigerian Market with just one month's production. In other words most African countries are not large enough to support major industries. To have these industries we must plan them on a sub-regional and regional basis. This is a crucial point that Africa has been making. This report is silent on it.

4. Action by the International Community

The next issue has to do with action by the international community, (pages 78-94 of the Report). Here the main areas of concern are:

i) international participation,

ii) international commodity cooperation,

iii) access to foreign markets

iv) resources.

In its recommendation promoting African international participation in the world trading system the report is curiously silent on African participation in commodity trading, that is international commodity exchanges. These are the markets that determine the prices for our products. If we are to be fair in talking about international co-operation, just as African countries used to participate in international commodity agreements so they also have a role in commodity exchanges because this is where our prices are determined.

In the area of international co-operation the report is curiously silent about international commodity agreements, ICAs. It says that ICAs should be encouraged as they are good for promoting Africa's commodity trade. But it is silent on the ICAs that have been scrapped or suspended. For example, the International Coffee Agreement has been suspended, the one for cocoa is not operational and almost all the others are in limbo. Yet this report makes no recomendation about revitalizing these commodity agreements. How can we talk about international commodity cooperation without reviving them?

With respect to access to foreign markets, the report says this should be the long-term objective of the industrialized countries. I want to emphasize long-term. The prominent economist, J. M. Keynes, said that in the long run we are all dead. The question is, what are the industrialized countries to do about access to their markets? In economic analysis, the long run starts from about ten years, from the year 2000. What is to happen between now and then? Specifically, what about the protectionist policies presently in place in the U.S., the EEC and so on? What are the implications of Europe 1992? There's hardly a page in this report on the implications on Africa's commodity trade. Along with the present Lome IV Convention between the EEC and the ACP countries (Africa, Caribbean and the Pacific), how will Africa get greater access to markets in 1992?

The Lome Convention suggests that fairly soon many of the commodities that African countries now export to the EEC, especially tropical produce, will in future come from Latin America and Asia. Africa will lose those markets. This is the reason for the anxious dialogues which the Francophone countries have been having with France . This report is silent on this and we are surprised that the representatives of Francophone countries, including the Ivory Coast, signed this report. I am sure they didn't undertand what they were signing.

Nowhere does the report say anything about the dangers to Africa and the possible losses resulting from the Uruguay Round of GATT.

I am sure that the committee headed by Micheal Fraser could not have been so ignorant as to not know that Africa would lose out. This is a very serious omission. There is no excuse for their failure to analyse the implications of Europe 1992 and the Uruguay Round and propose measures to protect Africa from them both .

On the question of resources, the report has four categories: aid, external debt, compensatory finance and additional resources.

On foreign aid it is silent on a fact mentioned repeatedly by the Third U.N. Development Decade: that very few advanced countries have been fufilling the target of providing 0.7–1% of their GNP in foreign Aid. As Prof. Timbhagen of Holland has argued, there is a curious relationship with the African Debt Crisis. If this target had been fulfilled, the amount of aid would be almost equal to the total size of Africa's foreign debt. In other words, Africa would not have got into debt.

On external debt the report asks for a moratorium of 3-10 years. What would be the effect on Africa's trade? Our main export commodities are coffee, cocoa and tea. They take about 7-8 years to produce. A moritorium of 3 years would mean that new trees would be only half grown by the time repayments were due to resume . The recommendation is conservative. Africa has been asking for a minimum of a ten year moratorium. Of course Africa's other demands, such as the cancellation of the debts of least developed countries, which even the OECD and Commonwealth have accepted partially, and the freezing of interest rates on remaining debt are not addressed. We have rejected debt rescheduling and debt refinancing because this brings no relief for Africa. It just postpones the evil day and makes it worse.

On the question of compensatory finance the report makes no provision for additional resources. The compensatory finance provided is tied to the CCFF (The Commodity Compensatory Financing Facility) and its structural adjustment facility ESAF. The CCFF, of which African countries have been complaining, is not adequate. And so to tie compensatory finance to that is no solution. Then the ASAF: in May 1990 it was found that of the $10 million available, less than 20% had been allocated, to a total of only 10 countries. And yet ASAF was to end in December 1990. The report is curiously silent on the International Commodity Fund, a form of compensatory finance that has been established through pressure by African countries. Since its establishment, African countries have been complaining that it is too small relative to Africa's requirements and that there are too many preconditions which they have to satisfy in order to get money from it.

Finally the report talks about additional resources and I will only mention two . On page 91 it quotes the World Bank LTPS : "Africa's savings gap, the difference between investment and savings, would be about $27 billion", about 9% of GDP. The report claims this is the amount of additional resources required by African countries. That is not true. The OAU and the ECA have made a separate calculation of additional resources needed, which would be equal not just to the savings gap but to the savings gap plus the trade gap. Even if you only take the larger of the two gaps, the figure is around $55 billion. The question is – why didn't this report use Africa's own figures? Why did it prefer the World Bank's view? And why the silence on the trade gap? This is a report on trade – why does it prefer the savings gap?

The report recommends three sources for additional resources, From the first it says African countries could get about $0.5 –1.0 billion; from the second source , ODA soft loans, it could get $4.6 billion and from the third source, $15 billion. If you add the three together Africa will get $20.6 billion dollars and yet the report says elsewhere that additional resources of $27 billion are required. Where is the balance of $6.4 billion to come from? Who will provide it?

In conclusion, I find this to be an extremely unsatisfactory report.

CLOSING ADDRESS

Tchouta Moussa, Deputy Executive Secretary of ECA..

We are pleased to have hosted this Workshop of the Institute for African Alternatives on the World Bank's Sub-Saharan Africa: From Crisis to Sustainable Growth – A Long-term Perspective Study (LTPS), the Uruguay Round of GATT and the Fraser Report on Africa's Commodity Problems.

As you are aware, the ECA is a regional member of the UN system that has been encouraging the participation of NGOs in the processes of recovery, development and democratization. It is to reinforce this promotion of NGO activities that the ECA jointly organised the February 1990 conference with other UN agencies, African governments and NGOs (both South and North) that produced the African Charter for Popular Participation in Development. This Charter was adopted by the OAU at its last summit and this underscores the OAUs endorsement of the important role of NGOs in Africa's accelerated recovery and transformation.

The Workshop's objectives included the promotion of public attention and discourse on these documents, encouragement of their critical evaluation by African people whose welfare and interests will be fundamentally affected by the implementation of these programmes and proposing Africa's alternatives to them. Your intention was to provide broad popular and intellectual support to African countries on the issues raised in these documents. These indeed are the duties of African academics and NGOs on our continent.

I understand that you highlighted the merits and major shortcomings of the LTPS, especially with respect to 'new generation SAPs', low projected growth rates, excessive reliance on market forces and the call for a Global Coalition for Africa. You stressed the possible losses and dangers of the Uruguay Round of GATT to Africa's trade and development and endorsed Africa's Common Position on the Fraser Report.

The conclusions and recommendations of your Workshop will promote public understanding and assist policy formulation in these areas.

This should promote the development of our self-confidence as Africans in our capacity to articulate our own policies and programmes; a self-confidence which has been so severely damaged by persistent foreign displacement of African initiatives. As we Africans rise to relaunch and lead the development process in the 1990s, we must demonstrate self-confidence in our ability to formulate and evaluate programmes and pursue the implementation of our own programmes, no matter what Africa's detractors may say or do.

This is the bitter lesson of the non-implementation of the Lagos Plan of Action because of the diversionary tactics of those who cannot see anything good coming from Africa.

I wish to congratulate you all for the initiative shown in organising this workshop. We hope other academics and NGOs will emulate your worthy example.